S0-BNK-009

The Academic
Job Search Handbook

Third Edition

The Academic Job Search Handbook

Mary Morris Heiberger and Julia Miller Vick

THIRD EDITION

PENN

UNIVERSITY OF PENNSYLVANIA PRESS

Philadelphia

Copyright © 1992, 1996, 2001 Mary Morris Heiberger and Julia Miller Vick
All rights reserved
Printd in the United States of America on acid-free paper

10   9   8   7   6   5   4   3   2

Published by
University of Pennsylvania Press
Philadelphia, Pennsylvania 19104-4011

Library of Congress Cataloging-in-Publication Data
Heiberger, Mary Morris.
  The academic job search handbook / Mary Morris Heiberger and Julia Miller
Vick.—3rd ed.
      p.   cm.
  Includes bibliographical references and index.
  ISBN 0-8122-1778-0 (pbk.: alk. paper)
  1. College teachers—Employment—United States—Handbooks, manuals, etc.
2. College teachers—Selection and appointment— United States—Handbooks,
manuals, etc.   I. Vick, Julia Miller.   II. Title.
LB2331.72 .H45   2001
650.14′088′372—dc21   2001027489

Contents

IV. Conducting the Search

V. After You Take the Job

VI. Thinking About the Expanded Job Market

Appendices

Acknowledgments

The first version of this handbook was written in consultation with our original Graduate Faculty Placement Council, an advisory group to the University of Pennsylvania's Career Planning and Placement Service (now Career Services). Its members contributed their vast experience to and carefully commented on the document. For years faculty members have generously shared their insight and experience at programs we have organized for graduate students. Dr. Janice Madden, former Vice Provost for Graduate Education at the University of Pennsylvania (now Director of Graduate Studies, Fels Center of Government and Professor of Regional Science/Sociology/Real Estate), co-sponsored and was an unfailing supporter of these events, as well as a frequent speaker at them. Dr. Dwight L. Jaggard, Professor of Electrical Engineering, and Dr. Walter Licht, Professor of History, frequently and enthusiastically participated in our programs while serving as University of Pennsylvania Graduate Deans in their respective schools. They sharpened our understanding and encouraged us to continue to look for the commonalities in the academic experience. It is impossible to thank all the other speakers here individually, but we are well aware that but for them this book could not exist. Graduate students, postdoctoral fellows, graduate alumni, and junior faculty members have discussed their own job searches with us; they have broadened our awareness of the range of what may happen and increased our ability to predict what is likely to happen.

We are particularly grateful to those graduate students and alumni of the University of Pennsylvania and other institutions who shared their sample job-hunting materials with us. Because we promised them anonymity, we cannot thank them here by name. However, their generosity has provided what many will find to be the most useful part of this book.

Our colleagues at the Career Services at the University of Pennsylvania have been consistently encouraging and tolerant of the disruption writing a book imposes on a busy student-services office. We feel fortunate that its director, Patricia Rose, has been uniformly enthusiastic about and supportive of this project.

The current edition has benefited greatly from the careful reading and suggestions of colleagues at the Office of Postdoctoral Programs, School of Medicine, University of Pennsylvania, Dr. Trevor M. Penning, Director and Associate Dean for Postdoctoral Research Training, and Janet Zinser, Associate Director. We also thank Dr. Judy M. Dacus, Instructor, Department of Biological Sciences, Lousiana State University, for her reading from the perspective of community college hiring. Mamiko Hada did a meticulous job of revising the information on scholarly associations. We are grateful to Jennifer Shenk for her extraordinary copyediting.

We thank all those who served as original members of the Graduate Faculty Placement Council: Dr. Beth E. Allen, Economics (now at the University of Minnesota); Dr. Elijah Andersen, Sociology; Dr. Fred L. Block, Sociology (now at the University of California, Davis); Dr. Lee V. Cassanelli, History; Dr. Peter Conn, English (now Deputy Provost); Dr. Terry H. Fortune, Physics; Dr. Stephen Gale, Regional Science; Dr. Marsha I. Lester, Chemistry; Ms. Maggie Morris (now Maggie McCartney), Graduate Division, School of Arts and Sciences (now Director, Office of Research and Funded Projects, California State University, Dominguez Hills); Dr. Edward N. Pugh, Jr., Psychology; Dr. Eugene K. Wolf, Music; and Dr. Sally H. Zigmond, Biology. We are particularly grateful to Dr. Beth Allen, who generously shared materials on deciding where to apply.

In addition, we owe a particular debt to those who read and commented upon the draft of the first edition of this book: Dr. Peter Conn, English (now Deputy Provost); Dr. Gregory Farrington, Engineering (now President, Lehigh University); Dr. Terry H. Fortune, Physics; and Dr. Ross A. Webber, Management (now emeritus).

We want to thank our colleagues and families for their interest in and support of this project.

Patricia Smith, former Acquisitions Editor at the University of Pennsylvania Press (now Editor, Silhouette Romances), first suggested we publish this book. We learned a great deal from her and particularly want to thank her.

Introduction to the Third Edition

The Academic Job Search Handbook is designed to be a comprehensive guide to what is often a needlessly bewildering process. It is written to help new Ph.D.s, as well as junior faculty members who are changing positions, benefit from the experience of those who have successfully navigated the academic market. For many years we have worked with doctoral students at our own institution and, recently, corresponded with Ph.D.s nationally who read our on-line column for *The Chronicle of Higher Education.* We have also spoken with faculty and administrators of scholarly societies across disciplines about all aspects of the academic job search, as well as with graduate career advisors at other institutions. We have found that, while people tend to feel their own fields are unique, there are fundamental similarities in effective searches, whether one is a scientist, a social scientist, a humanist, or a researcher in a professional field. This book discusses those aspects of the search that must be managed by Ph.D.s in both the arts and sciences and the professional disciplines.

The book begins with an overview of academic careers and institutional structures. It then takes you step by step through the application process, from establishing relationships with advisors years before going on the market to making the most of a new position. Steps discussed include positioning yourself in the market, learning about job listings, preparing vitas, cover letters, and other application materials, discussing plans with those who will recommend you, participating in conferences, and negotiating offers. Sample written materials, a timetable for your search, and an appendix of scholarly and professional associations are included.

Even if you are particularly interested in a few specific topics, we suggest that you read the book in its entirety. If you do, you will begin to see how advice on one topic is related to advice on another. If you understand the logic of the approach suggested in the situations we do discuss, you will be able to improvise effectively when you encounter a new situation.

Each discipline also has its own customs. What is "right" is frequently what is done in one's own field. Thus, this guide should never replace the specific conventions of your discipline. You may find useful advice on job-hunting from your national professional association. Faculty members in your own field will always be able to give the best perspective on your search. In job hunting, as in anything else, unanimity is rare. When expert advice conflicts, we hope that the handbook will have given you a perspective from which to form your own judgment.

Since the *Handbook* was first published in 1992, and even since the second edition in 1996, there have been several changes in higher education, all of them resulting in increased pressure on candidates in the academic market. Cutbacks in public funding for higher education have put pressure on all institutions, private as well as public. Furthermore, as the cost of educating students continues to increase, pressure to reemphasize teaching has been generated by parents, legislators, employers, and students themselves. However, the pressure to compete for research grants has also, if anything, intensified, and the amount of research required to achieve tenure has increased. Institutions have shown increasing reliance on contract rather than tenure-track positions, and distance learning is affecting the delivery of education in ways whose impact we are only beginning to see. Additionally, for-profit education is beginning to compete with traditional institutions of higher education.

Well-qualified candidates still get jobs, but they have to work harder and longer (over a period of years) to do so. We hope that the revised version reflects this reality, while still encouraging and assisting those who truly want to be scholars, teachers, and researchers to persist in pursuing their goals.

In spite of increased competition, how candidates should look for jobs in this market has not substantially changed, so much of our original advice remains the same. However, we have added some new materials.

A new chapter in this edition and some of its sample written materials also reflect the reality that many people, while having an academic career as their first choice, are also considering other options as they pursue their academic search. We're pleased to see that many scholarly associations are acknowledging the possibility that scholarly skills can be put to good use outside of the academy, as can be seen in many of the links provided in our appendix of scholarly associations.

Throughout, this edition acknowledges that many candidates are competing for jobs in the one growth area in higher education, community colleges. We have included more examples from experienced candidates seeking a second or third position, because so many experienced people have told us they read the book. We hope their materials will also help recent graduates see what to expect a few years down the road. We've added more discussion for those in scientific and other technical fields and extended the discussion of considerations for dual career couples. Virtually all the sample job-search materials are new, including more examples of the "teaching philosophies" now commonly asked for in job ads.

We hope that this revised volume is helpful. Academic careers still offer the opportunity for intensely satisfying and productive work. We hope that by clarifying some of the processes by which positions are obtained, we can reduce some of the anxiety and uncertainty of the job-hunting process so that candidates can get on with their chosen teaching and research.

Part I
What You Should Know
Before You Start

Chapter 1
The Structure of Academic Careers

You will be entering the job market at a time when higher education is subject to intense financial constraints, self-scrutiny, external assessment, competition, and accelerating technological change. One of the safest statements that can be made about your academic career, which may well extend over the next forty years, is that it will probably be unlike those of your predecessors. Nevertheless, you are entering the market as it exists now, so it is important to understand how academic jobs have traditionally been organized.

The system of higher education in the United States is bewildering in its variety and complexity. Unlike many countries, the United States has no national, in the sense of federally funded, universities. Its major universities, both private and state-funded, house faculties of arts and sciences and major professional schools. There are also small publicly funded institutions, and that peculiarly American institution, the four-year college, which is usually, but not always, private. Privately funded institutions are frequently secular, but are sometimes funded by religious institutions, whose religious influence on campus varies from nonexistent to omnipresent. Two-year community colleges constitute an increasingly important segment of higher education. Universities run as for-profit businesses are new, but growing rapidly.

Both colleges and universities (or campuses of major universities) may enjoy either regional or national reputations. As a general rule, universities of national reputation place the most emphasis upon research as the criterion of success for faculty members. Teaching is most likely to be emphasized at less prestigious universities and at four-year colleges, although four-year colleges of national reputation also require substantial research of their faculty members.

Both student and faculty life are affected by conditions of faculty employment. At some institutions, nearly all faculty are full-time. Others use many part-time instructors. Faculty and other staff members at some institutions are unionized. Where unions exist, membership may be high across the board, or it may vary widely from school to school and department to department.

Career Ladders

Given the variety of institutions, the similarity of their promotional structures is surprising. The structure of academic hiring has been dominated by the tenure system, with a fairly orderly ladder that at most institutions leads from assistant professor to associate professor (with tenure) to full professor. This "tenure track" route leads to status as a standing member of the faculty with full rights of participation in institutional decision making, and what is close to a lifetime guarantee of a job, barring economic upheaval or conviction for criminal activity. Tenure is coming under increasing scrutiny by state legislatures and boards of trustees and a few institutions have dismantled their tenure systems. For now, however, achieving it is still the goal of almost everyone who first accepts a faculty postition.

Tenure-track positions have been supplanted in many institutions by a variety of positions conceived of as temporary: instructorships, lectureships, visiting and research assistant/associate professorships. These have always existed for a variety of institutional reasons: to cover heavy teaching loads for introductory courses in a department that does not have enough, or any, graduate students to meet the demand; to replace a faculty member who is on sabbatical; to enable individuals able to secure research funds to be associated with a university.

Now they are primarily created as institutional attempts to save the costs of tenure-track positions. In addition to struggling with government cutbacks in funding for higher education, colleges and universities have to deal with the effects of the recent "uncapping" of a mandatory retirement age. By federal law, institutions no longer can require faculty members to retire merely because they have reached a certain age. Many tenured faculty members of traditional retirement age (who also tend to be the highest-salaried members of their departments) are choosing to continue teaching, thus adding greatly to schools' personnel costs and providing fewer entry opportunities for new Ph.D.s. Not uncommonly, when a faculty member does retire, his or her expensive tenure-track position is converted by the institution into a non-tenure-track position.

Even though these positions may be held by the same individual and renewed over a period of several years, they are best thought of by job candidates as temporary, because they are outside the school's structure of permanent employment. In many cases holding such a position does not offer an inside track for permanent employment with the department, because if a tenure-track position becomes available a national search will be conducted. Most candidates holding these temporary positions continue to compete for tenure-track positions, so that even assistant professor slots will draw applications from experienced Ph.D.s., as well as new ones.

Hiring and promotion have tended to become less "genteel" and more market-driven in the recent decade, with no sign that the trend will be reversed. It has become less likely that candidates will obtain positions through a few phone calls made by an advisor, more likely that jobs will be nationally advertised, and more likely that institutions will compete for candidates in "hot" fields using salaries, reduced teaching loads, and special research facilities to attract candidates.

Paths to Academic Administration

Educational institutions, even small ones, are also complex organizations with managerial structures. They have physical plants, staff, investments, and budgets in at least the millions of dollars. Therefore they need the same sorts of managers as are found in the business world. Many of these individuals do not have academic backgrounds.

The management of academic programs, on the other hand, is a responsibility usually held by those who have followed an academic career path. A faculty member who is interested in academic administration typically begins by taking on a greater than ordinary share of administrative and committee tasks within his or her department and institution. A frequent path might lead from department chair to dean to provost, usually the chief academic officer. Some institutions choose their president from those who have followed this route. Others do not, looking for a president with substantial experience in a profession, business, or government, or on the business side of managing a university.

The climb to academic administration generally begins after at least obtaining tenure, and, more likely, as a full professor. Individuals who are strongly drawn to administrative activity can certainly find entry-level positions with good possibilities for promotion. It is likely, however, that they will have a lower ceiling on career advancement than those who have begun as faculty members.

Movement Between Institutions During a Career

In some fields, particularly science and engineering, up to several years of postdoctoral experience are required in order to obtain a tenure-track slot at a major research institution, so people in those fields almost inevitably will change institutions early in their careers.

Despite tenure's presumption of lifetime employment, faculty members in all fields increasingly move between institutions in the course of a career. Typical occasions of moves may include not getting tenure at one institution; being "lured away" by another that is trying to build its department, at a higher salary or rank; and responding to a job opportunity for a spouse or partner.

To some extent, there is a national hierarchy of colleges and universities, roughly correlated with the research reputations of their faculty members and their selectivity in admitting students. In addition, there is something of a national hierarchy of departments, based on approximately the same standards. For example, an institution of generally average quality may sometimes house one of the premier departments in a given discipline.

It is generally easier to move from an institution of higher status to one of lower status than to move in the other direction. To some extent, this is a function of "name recognition." In addition, the most prominent institutions generally provide the best facilities for research on the part of their faculty members, both in terms of equipment and libraries, and reduced teaching loads. People at these institutions generally have more opportunities for the kind of research that will lead to additional opportunities. Therefore, candidates usually aim as high as possible in the choice of a first academic position.

Does this mean that a candidate who does not begin an academic career at a major research institution may never have a chance to be on the faculty of one? Of course not. Particularly in the tight job market of recent years, candidates have taken the best positions they were offered, continued to do research, and moved to other institutions within a few years. They have been able to make these moves through visibility generated from research, publication, and participation in national professional or scholarly organizations. In recent years in many fields new Ph.D.s who aspire to positions at major research institutions have needed up to several years of postdoctoral fellowships or research appointments in order to continue to build their record of research to a competitive level. It is the case, however, that if an individual does not move to an institution or department of national reputation within the first few years of a career, whatever the form of appointment, he or she becomes increasingly less likely to do so.

Some movement is also possible between academic and nonacademic institutions. This is particularly likely to be the case in professional schools, in which candidates may join the faculty at a senior level after achieving a distinguished record of accomplishment in the profession. Scientific and technical areas have also seen increasing movement between academic and industrial research settings.

However, transferability of credentials between academic and nonacademic settings varies greatly from field to field. It is a good idea to seek advice from senior individuals on both "sides" so that you do not make a major career move without being aware of its probable implications. You may need, for example, to learn how long scholars in your field can refrain from pursuing active research before they risk being unable to resume it with any credibility.

Academic Lives

The kind of position one gets, and at what institution, will have important ramifications for one's life. Research universities may demand research conducted at practically nonstop intensity, and careers may be tied to continuously obtaining new grants. Four-year colleges may expect faculty members to spend lots of time with individual students outside of class, perhaps even opening one's home to them. Short-term contracts may require frequent relocation, perhaps nationally. The period between obtaining a tenure-track position and obtaining tenure requires constant juggling of priorities as it presents so many demands. Despite their heavy workloads, academics have more freedom to structure their own time than practically anyone else in the economy. For some people, this is the great advantage of the career path; for others, it is a source of stress.

Academics, like other people, establish long-term relationships, have children, buy houses, care for elderly parents, try to make time for hobbies and community service, and hope to have some retirement income. Since academics are particularly likely to bring work home, boundaries between work and the rest of life are often blurred. When you plan your academic career, inevitably you're planning the rest of your life as well.

Chapter 2
Hiring from the Institution's Point of View

Just as your vita presents the public face of your qualifications in a simple, organized form, without revealing the full complexity of your individual life, an advertised position is the public presentation of an outcome of complex negotiations within a department and possibly within an institution.

It will generally be impossible for you, as a job candidate, to have a full understanding of what goes on behind the scenes. Even if you are fortunate enough to have an inside contact who can give you additional perspective, it is still extremely unlikely that you will know everything about the hiring decision. Thus, throughout the job search process, you will need to present yourself in the strongest fashion possible without tying yourself into knots trying to second guess the institution that has advertised the position.

However, here are some of the considerations that might be at work.

Defining and Advertising a Position

It may be fairly easy for a department to obtain approval and funding for a renewable lectureship or sabbatical replacement position. When a tenure-track position is listed, however, it reflects efforts by a department to maintain or strengthen its hiring position vis-à-vis other departments in the school. In today's financially stringent climate, approval to fill a position that has been vacated is not granted routinely. The department that has lost a staff member must defend to its dean the necessity of replacing the position. Meanwhile other departments are lobbying to expand their staff. If the hiring department has been given a new position, that very fact reflects even more intense departmental lobbying.

The definition of the position more frequently reflects discussion internal to the department. In some cases the definition is obvious: the department absolutely must replace a faculty member with a particular expertise. Perhaps, too, the department has a long-range plan that calls for increasing areas of strength in some orderly fashion. At other times, there may be dissension within the department about how the new position should be defined. Some want the department to move in one direction, some in another. The debate is resolved to the point necessary to define and advertise a position, but it does not necessarily mean that everyone has been convinced.

Further complicating the situation is the tendency of departments in recent years to advertise positions simultaneously at the assistant and associate professor levels, leaving the area of specialization entirely open. In that case, the department has clearly chosen to "see who's out there," planning to make an offer to whoever in its view is the best candidate. New Ph.D.s are often unnecessarily frightened by an ad that mentions positions at both levels. The hiring department will not compare a new Ph.D. to a senior faculty member. The new Ph.D. will be compared to other new Ph.D.s, the senior faculty member to other senior faculty members, and an offer will be made to the individual who both is the best candidate relative to his or her peer group and can best fit the needs of the department.

Implications for Candidates

A department that has gone to considerable trouble to get approval to hire for a position will not take kindly to applicants who seem to view it as a second-best alternative to be abandoned as soon as something better comes along. Therefore, it is important that you as a candidate convey a serious interest in the position throughout the search process. Don't get bogged down in self-comparisons to imagined other candidates. Concentrate on communicating what you have to offer. The position may be even more appropriate and desirable than you realize.

Screening Candidates

All faculty members in a small department may be involved in hiring, whereas in a larger one the logistics of managing the search, and a good deal of decision making, may be delegated to a search committee. In some cases the committee may include a student representative. In most hiring bodies, there will be some members of the group who are intensely interested in who is ultimately hired and who take the process very seriously; others who take participation seriously, but view it as an obligation that interferes with things they would rather be doing; and, possibly, an individual who wishes he or she were elsewhere and who participates without giving the process full attention.

The hiring group will read through the materials submitted in response to the advertisement. At this stage candidates, of necessity, get the least careful screening, because it simply is not possible to do an in-depth evaluation of what may be up to several hundred sets of materials sent in response to an advertisement. Individuals in the hiring group are probably not yet wedded to the candidates they prefer, because most of these are still abstractions, presented on paper.

Therefore, if someone asks the group to pay special attention to a candidate at this stage, the request is likely to be honored. The request may take the form of a phone call from a dean who says, "X is the spouse of Y, who is department Z's top choice. We'll lose her unless we can make an offer to him. See what you think." It may take the form of a phone call from a department member's former dissertation advisor who says, "Dr. L. is the best student the department has had in the last five years and she is seriously interested in this job. Can you be sure to look at her application carefully?"

In some cases, those who are to be interviewed at a convention or who are to be directly invited to campus for an interview will be chosen from the materials sent initially. However, as the money available to bring candidates for campus interviews tightens, departments are often trying to narrow the pool of candidates to a smaller group, who will be asked to provide additional materials such as dissertation chapters or articles and/or to have initial screening interviews by phone.

Implications for Candidates

As will be discussed in detail in later chapters, make all the materials used in your application clear and accessible, even to someone who is not a specialist in your area. Don't be afraid to be slightly redundant. For example, if your cover letter repeats some of the material in your vita, someone who does not pay full attention to one may pick up key points from the other.

Consider asking a senior faculty member from your Ph.D.-granting institution whether he or she knows anyone at the school to which you are applying, and then ask for a phone call on your behalf. This call can draw attention to your candidacy and help keep your application in the group of those chosen for further examination.

Once you apply for a position, be prepared to submit additional supporting materials promptly and/or to be interviewed by phone on very short notice.

Interviewing

In some fields, departments interview many candidates at a national convention and then invite a smaller group for second interviews on campus. In other fields, the campus interview is the first and only one. Once the interviewing process begins, issues of personality, style, and the department's own history begin to come into play, in unpredictable fashion. Most departments have their own histories of hiring "successes" and "mistakes." Naturally they will attempt to repeat one and avoid the other. Therefore, statements made by a candidate during an interview may have resonances unknown to the candidate. For example, if your remarks closely parallel those of a candidate hired two years ago, they will probably be heard differently depending on the current consensus as to whether hiring that candidate was a coup or a mistake.

As a candidate, you are unlikely to have a full understanding of power and influence within the department. Obviously, you must be chosen by the hiring committee and approved by the chairperson. In addition, however, there may exist individuals of sufficient influence that the department may be reluctant to hire anyone to whom they strongly object. In some institutions, particularly community colleges, nondepartmental faculty members and administrators are significantly involved in hiring.

Implications for Candidates

When your interview is scheduled, find out with whom you'll meet during the course of your visit. Get all the firsthand information about the department and institution that you can possibly gather. However, you should recognize that you are likely to gain, at best, only a partial understanding of the departmental dynamics. Therefore, don't try to second guess your interviewers. Again, concentrate on the clear communication of what you have to say.

Decision Making

After a small number of candidates have been invited to campus for an interview, the department must decide to whom to offer the position. Sometimes the choice is simple; sometimes it is agonizing. Faced with the real people who have interviewed for the position, rather than the "ideal" represented by the ad, the department may need to make very concrete trade-offs. What if the candidate who is ideal in terms of the qualities described in the ad has charmed one-half of the department and totally alienated the other? What if no one really fits the job that was envisioned, but one candidate seems outstanding in every other respect?

The department must make its decisions, knowing that job offers and acceptances are occurring over the space of a few months. It knows the largest salary that it can pay, and it knows that it must give its first-choice candidate at least a week or two to decide whether to accept the offer. It may believe that the first-choice candidate is extremely unlikely to accept the position, and that the second-choice candidate, also very good, is likely to accept, but only if the position is offered within the next few weeks. Finally, if none of the candidates seem entirely satisfactory, the department must decide whether to leave the position vacant for a year and risk losing it to some kind of budgetary constraint, and reopen the search the following year.

Usually the department comes to a decision that balances competing priorities. Depending upon the department's style, a job may be offered to the candidate who has not alienated anyone, to the candidate who is most strongly backed by a few influential department members, to the candidate who appears most neutral in terms of some controversy that has split the department, or to a candidate chosen in a close vote. Depending on the institution, the department's decision will be endorsed by the administration or must be vigorously defended to it.

Implications for Candidates

Do your best to accept the fact that hiring is not usually a matter of choosing the "best" candidate by some set of abstract criteria, but of making a reasonable choice among valid, if competing, priorities, an inherently political process. Do your best, therefore, not to dismiss the process as somehow unethical. If each member of a hiring committee honestly thinks a different candidate is the best choice for the department, a decision must be made somehow. Unless it is to be settled by a duel or a flip of a coin, it must be decided through a negotiated process that acknowledges several factors not necessarily known to the candidates.

If you insist on thinking either that there is an obviously "best" candidate for every job and that every time that person has not been chosen an immoral decision has been made, or that hiring is a random process amounting to no more than the luck of the draw, you will diminish your own ability to understand the difference between what is and is not in your control. Worse, you risk becoming angry, bitter, or cynical and therefore approaching potential employers with a visible presumption that they will be unfair.

Approach a department as if you expect it to behave in a fair and reasonable fashion. Make it easy for those who would like to hire you to lobby for you, by being well prepared, by communicating an attitude of respect for everyone you meet during the course of a day, and by making all your

written application materials as clear and strong as you can. Let your enthusiasm for the position be obvious.

Keep a record of the people with whom you speak during each application. Even if you do go elsewhere, you can keep in touch with them, send papers to them, and cultivate them over the years. They may invite you back after you establish a reputation elsewhere.

Negotiation and Acceptance

Once a position is offered, there may be a brief period of negotiation about salary, terms of employment (for example, research facilities, or how many classes are to be taught in the first year), and time given the candidate to make a decision. Sometimes there will be delays, as the department must receive approval from a higher level before making a specific offer. Usually other finalists will be notified of a decision only after a candidate has definitely accepted a position.

Implications for Candidates

Understand that delays may be inevitable. However, if your own situation changes (for example, if you get another offer), do not hesitate to let the department know immediately. If you are turned down, it's natural to wonder why. Except in the unlikely event that you have a friend in the department, you're unlikely to find out. However, you may wish to ask for constructive feedback. If you do ask, concentrate your questions on what you might have done to strengthen your presentation, rather than on how the decision was made.

Was the Job Wired?

Sometimes, at the conclusion of a search, it is widely perceived that the advertised position was not truly open. There was a high probability at the outset that an offer would be made to someone who was already within the department; to someone whom the department had been wooing for the last few years; to a member of a group whose underrepresentation among faculty members was viewed as an intolerable situation; to a clone of those already in the department; and so on.

Implications for Candidates

Compete for every job you want as if you have a genuine chance of being offered it, whatever you guess or have been told. That way you best position yourself to take advantage of the uncertainty inherent in every hiring situation. Maybe the department does have a strong front-runner, but he or she will not accept the position in the end. Maybe you are very unlikely to get this job, but the campus interview you are offered will help you polish your interviewing skills so that you will do better at the next interview.

Remember that, even if you are not successful in getting a particular job, you have left behind an impression of abilities, talents, and personality. Frequently, faculty members will talk with colleagues at other schools about good candidates whom they interviewed but were not able to hire. Even if your interview at a particular school is unsuccessful, it can serve as good advertising, depending upon how you deal with the interview situation and, particularly, with any rejection.

When you are hired, there may well be disappointed candidates who think that you had some kind of unfair advantage, so try to be generous in your assessment of the decisions made by what are, by and large, well-intentioned people.

Part II
Planning and Timing
Your Search

Chapter 3
Becoming a Job Candidate:
The Timetable for Your Search

It is important to begin to prepare for your job search well before you finish your dissertation; in many fields it is also important to time the search to coincide with the completion of your dissertation. Many scientists, on the other hand, are competitive on the tenure-track market only after a few to several years of postdoctoral research. Think about your job search, your participation in scholarly organizations, and the completion of your dissertation or postdoctoral research as a unified whole. Most faculty members will advise you not to take a tenure-track position before your dissertation is completed. A strong logic informs that view. In a tight job market, candidates who have completed their degrees are likely to be chosen over those who have not. In addition, once you have accepted a position, you will gain tenure as a result of research done as a junior faculty member. If you begin your research by completing the dissertation, you will already be late by the tenure clock, and in the position of a student with several incompletes, who can never catch up with current work.

Funding considerations may force you to look for paid employment before your dissertation is completed. If this is the case, discuss the situation with faculty members in your department and choose the employment most conducive to finishing the dissertation.

Use the timetable below to plan your job search while completing your dissertation and participating in scholarly activities. Each suggested step is discussed in detail elsewhere in this book. If, by chance, you read it thinking, "I wish I had done some of these things last year," don't despair! Fill in the gaps as best you can. Certainly many people obtain positions without having conducted the "perfect" job search. However, if you see gaps in your preparation and do not do as well as you hope in the job market this year, you may find much more success if you go on the market again next year after better preparation.

Timetable for Applying for Jobs That Begin in September

Two Years Before

- Make sure all members of your dissertation committee are selected. Consider getting a December degree, which enables you to apply with "degree in hand." (Foreign nationals, however, should consider the visa implications of this timing.) Learn about conference dates and locations. Plan to attend and, if feasible, to give a presentation. Learn deadlines for submitting papers.
- Learn about all the important sources of job listings in your field. In some disciplines the job listings of one scholarly association cover almost everything. In other fields there may be multiple sources.
- Explore Internet resources and bookmark useful sites.
- Give thought to your long-range goals and consider the kinds of jobs you will wish to apply for. If your plans will have an impact on a spouse or partner, begin to talk with that person about geographic locations you will both consider acceptable.
- If you have the opportunity to do so, start to sit in on the talks and interviews of job candidates in your department. Think about what they do that does and doesn't work well. If your department allows students to review candidates' application materials, take advantage of this opportunity to see a large collection of them.
- Identify any relevant postdocs for which you may want to apply and learn their deadlines.
- If you are already in a postdoctoral position, you will want to seek a tenure-track position when you feel your research record is strong enough. Once you've decided you're ready to put yourself on the market, see "Fall, Twelve Months Before" below.
- Think about developing a backup plan. If it includes seeking nonacademic positions, start to educate yourself about the options. Two excellent resources are *Outside the Ivory Tower: A Guide for Academics Considering Alternative Careers* by Margaret Newhouse and *Nontraditional Careers in Science* by Karen Young Kreeger.

Summer, Fifteen Months Before

- Make sure your dissertation will be finished no later than the summer before the job begins, and preferably earlier. In many cases, hiring departments will not consider a candidate without a Ph.D. in hand.

- Discuss your plans with your advisor or postdoctoral supervisor and any others in the department who may be interested. If they don't think you will be ready to go on the market until the following year, consider their point of view very seriously. If you begin a new position and have not yet completed your dissertation, you will start off behind schedule in terms of the "tenure clock."
- Renew contacts with faculty members whom you may know at other institutions, letting them know of your progress and that you will be on the market soon.
- If you haven't already done so, set up a credentials file at your campus career center. Get letters of recommendation now from those with whom you will have no further significant contact.
- Collect all the materials you have that you might want to use or refer to as part of an application and make sure you can find them. Your collection could include reprints, copies of letters of commendation, newspaper articles about something you have done, syllabi you have prepared, and notes about things you want to remember to stress in a cover letter.
- Prepare your vita.
- If you think a Web site would enhance a candidacy in your field, develop one.
- Begin to prepare the additional written materials you will need in your search. You may be asked to provide an employer with an abstract or the first chapter of your dissertation; a research paper; a brief statement of your research plans or teaching philosophy; "evidence of successful teaching"; and sample syllabi.
- You may also be asked for a copy of your transcript. Be sure you know how to order it and how long it takes to fill a request.
- Consider giving a paper at a major conference in your field or submitting an article or articles to major journals in your field. Find out deadlines for calls for papers.
- If you will be applying for individual postdoctoral funding, obtain and begin to prepare postdoc applications. If you will be applying to work on someone's research grant, start to network with potential principal investigators.
- Think about what resources you will need to do your research as a faculty member. Begin to research ways of funding them. You may be asked about these issues in an interview.
- If you are also considering non-academic options, be aware that timetables for non-academic employment are different from academic ones, and usually more flexible. If an academic position is your first choice, concentrate on that search at this time.

Fall, Twelve Months Before

- Finalize your vita. (You may need to update it a few times during the year.) Complete additional supporting written materials.
- Arrange for letters of recommendation to be written by everyone who will support your search. Your advisor will probably update his or her letter as your dissertation progresses through its final stages.
- Find out whether jobs in your field typically require "teaching portfolios." Most fields don't, but if yours does, begin to prepare one. If you're in an art or design field, prepare the slides and portfolios you'll be asked to submit with applications. Don't forget to include samples of your students' work.
- Keep working on your dissertation or research project!
- Attend any programs on the academic job search that may be offered on campus or at conferences.
- Watch carefully for job listings and apply for everything that interests you. The first cover letters you write may take longer to compose than subsequent ones.
- Continue to keep in close touch with your advisor and other recommenders.
- Consider making a few direct inquiries at departments that particularly interest you (what you are most likely to discover in this way are non-tenure-track positions), if you can define reasonable criteria for selecting the departments.
- Review the literature in your field and subfield in preparation for interviews.
- Check to see that letters of application have been received by the departments to which you apply.
- Apply for postdocs.
- Investigate sources of funding for your research so that you can discuss your plans with hiring institutions.
- Plan ways to maintain your perspective and sense of humor during what can be a trying time. Consider exercise, having fun, seeking out campus resources, supporting others who are going through the same thing, and nurturing your own support network.

Eight Months Before

- Interviewers will ask you about your long-range research plans. Even if you are so immersed in your dissertation that you can't see beyond it at the moment, take time to give some thought to where your research will lead.

- Many conferences are held now. It is important to attend them and take advantage of the opportunity they provide for the formal and informal exchange of information.
- Prepare carefully for each interview. If you give a presentation as part of an interview day on campus, practice it in advance. Remember to send thank-you notes after each interview.
- Continue to look, apply, and interview for positions.
- This may well be a stressful time. Plan to take some breaks for activities or events that you consider relaxing and renewing.

Six Months Before

- Continue to apply and interview for positions, although most openings will have been announced by now.
- You may begin to get offers. If you feel you need more time to make a decision about an offer, don't hesitate to ask for it. You will, however, have to abide by whatever time frame you and the employer agree on for your decision. You don't need to be totally open with everyone at this stage, but you must be completely honest. When you do accept a position, consider your acceptance a binding commitment.
- If the offers you want are not coming in, don't think that you must take absolutely any job that is offered to you, whether you want it or not. The job market will come around again next year. Talk with your advisor and others about the best way to position yourself for next year's market, if necessary. You can also keep watching for one-year appointments, which are often announced later than tenure-track positions.
- After you have accepted a job, take time to thank everyone who has been helpful to you in the process.

Chapter 4
Deciding Where and When to Apply

Before you begin a job search, think about what kind of job you want and whether you are currently prepared to compete successfully for it. Study job ads to see what different types of institutions seem to require and use the information to help plan your next steps. If, realistically, you don't yet seem qualified to compete successfully for the jobs you really want, consider whether a postdoctoral position or fellowship, additional teaching experience, or anything else will position you for a successful search.

It's important to think about both your priorities and your realistic chances of achieving your goals. Even in a tight market where you feel options are limited, it's still useful to keep your sights on what you really want. The more articulate you can be about your plans and goals, the easier it will be for you to communicate with your advisor and others who will assist you in your job search, to prepare for interviewing, and to assess job offers.

Understanding the Market

You must know something about the job market before you begin your search. The more informed you are the better your search will be. The experience of graduate students a few years ahead of you in your department provides a very limited knowledge base. You need to do additional research to be conversant with the following:

- What is the hiring outlook in your discipline?
- What is the hiring outlook in your field of research?
- How broad is the market in your field? Opportunities may exist outside traditional departmental definitions. For example, although your degree is from an arts and sciences department, might you seek a position in a professional school (such as business, government, com-

munications)? Would a short-term experience, such as a postdoctoral appointment, increase your long-term options? Are you in a field, such as biomedical science, where a postdoc is all but required?
- How great is the competition for positions in your field at prestigious institutions? What is realistically required should you choose to compete for them? For example, would several publications in major journals be required?
- If you are in a highly specialized field, when and where are openings anticipated?

There are several ways you can obtain this information. Read articles in *The Chronicle of Higher Education*. Contact your scholarly association (see Appendix 1) for reports it may have produced about the market. Check to see whether your campus career center or graduate dean's office has records of the jobs taken by new Ph.D.s from your school. Talk with students in your department who are on the market or recent graduates who have new faculty positions. Above all, talk regularly with your department chair, advisor, and other faculty members about the job market in your field.

Deciding Where to Apply

Institutional Characteristics

Are you willing or eager to consider jobs at:

- A public or private institution?
- A large university or a small four-year teaching college or community college?
- A school with a distinctive institutional personality, such as a women's college, an institution with a strong religious affiliation, or a school offering an "innovative curriculum"?
- An institution that emphasizes research over teaching or one that emphasizes teaching over research? A competitive job market has enabled institutions that formerly emphasized only one of these things to require both; however, "teaching" and "research" institutions still may be distinguished from each other.
- A place that demands or offers heavy involvement in the life of the school (usually a teaching college) or one in which your major identification will be with your department?
- A highly selective institution or one that prides itself on offering educational opportunities to a broad section of the community?

- An institution where the faculty is unionized or one where individual salaries are market-driven?
- An institution that compensates new faculty members with salary or one that compensates them with prestige?
- A U.S. institution or one in another country?
- A for-profit university?

Departmental Characteristics

Do you prefer:

- Many colleagues in your field of research or an opportunity to be the inhouse expert in your field?
- Opportunity to and expectation that you will socialize with others in the department or an atmosphere that encourages solely professional involvement?
- An emphasis on graduate or on undergraduate teaching?
- A department in which you would be the first person of your social background ever hired, or one in which you feel most people are like you?
- A department with a specific orientation ("traditional," "radical," "applied") or one whose faculty members take a variety of approaches?
- A department where teaching occurs mainly in seminars or one where classes are primarily large lectures?
- A department that emphasizes research or one that emphasizes teaching? Think about what kind of facilities you need to carry out your own research plans.
- A department with a hierarchical structure or one that emphasizes participatory decision making?

Geographic Considerations

- Is it important to you to be in a rural, small city, suburban, or urban environment?
- Does your research require resources that are available in limited geographic locations?
- Can you work and live comfortably in any region of the country?
- Will you need to limit the geographic range of your search, or find an institution near an airport, because of personal considerations, such as the career plans of a partner, a child's education, or the need to be near a relative who is ill?

- Will you look only in the United States or will you expand your search to other countries? Are you able to teach in a language other than English?

Additional Personal Considerations

Additional idiosyncratic personal considerations may be important in your job search. Even if you are the only candidate in the world who will choose one position over another because it will give you the most opportunity and time to use your pilot's license, take this preference into consideration if it is important to you.

How Competitive Are You?

Be realistic in evaluating the type of institution where you will be able and willing to do what is necessary to attain tenure.

- In some fields, it is very important to be able to obtain funding for your own research. Do you feel willing and able to do this?
- Are you able to resist pressure from your own departmental culture to apply only to certain kinds of institutions?
- What balance do you want to strike between career-related features and nonprofessional aspects of a job? For example, would you take a position at a highly prestigious institution at which you would need to work nearly all your waking hours in order to have a reasonable chance of obtaining tenure?
- Do you see a discrepancy between your ability and willingness to perform in your first job and your ability to obtain it? For example, are you highly productive in research and publication and very awkward in oral presentations and conversations? In that case, work to improve your job-hunting skills instead of letting them limit your job search, because your job-hunting ability can always improve if you are willing to give it practice and attention. On the other hand, if you interview extremely well but seriously doubt your ability or willingness to perform the level of research required to get tenure, don't talk yourself into a job whose demands you may not want or be able to meet. The tenure clock usually starts the minute you accept a tenure-track position. If you feel you will be unable to do what will be required to achieve tenure, you will surely face another, possibly more difficult, job search down the road.

If You Are Applying for Postdocs

- Why are you choosing to do a postdoc? Is your field one where post-doc experience is usually required?
- Do you want to use your postdoctoral experience to increase your expertise in your dissertation area or to broaden your background?
- Will you do your postdoc in a large, top research institution or in a smaller school?
- What qualities do you plan to look for in the supervisor who will serve as your mentor? How do you plan to assess those qualities?
- What type of facilities and other resources are required for the type of research you want to do?
- How will you distinguish between the postdoctoral positions which amount to little more than serving as ill-paid research assistants and those which provide a strong basis for an independent scientific career?

When to Look

Because most jobs are advertised about a year before they are to begin, you will probably start your job search while you are still finishing your dissertation. Be realistic about when you will finish. It is crucial that you discuss with your advisor when to begin the search, because he or she will be knowledgeable about the advisability of being a candidate with an unfinished dissertation as opposed to one with the degree in hand. That is the most important factor in determining when to start looking.

On the other hand, if you are in a field with very few annual openings, and a good job is announced before you are entirely ready to apply, you and your advisor may decide that it is a good idea for you to accelerate your search. If you are in the first year of a postdoc with a two-year commitment and the perfect job opportunity comes along, you're in a difficult situation. You probably must discuss it with your supervisor, at least by the time you're invited for an interview, at which point the person will almost certainly find out about your application.

If it looks as if you will finish in a year in which very few openings are available, plan to search for good interim opportunities while you conduct the academic job search. Many postdoctoral and other fellowship opportunities, like academic positions, have very early deadlines for application. Don't wait until you find you have no job offers before you apply. Some faculty positions will continue to be listed throughout the academic year, so, while you must begin your search early, it may continue over several months.

If you are an international student, you should find out if there are visa considerations that might affect the timing of your search and the date when you might prefer to have your degree awarded. Start working on this task early to avoid problems or delays that might prevent an institution from offering you a job later on, or that might compromise your ability to remain long-term in the United States if that is your desire. If your campus has an office that offers good visa and immigration advising, use it. If not, consult a reputable immigration attorney.

Discussing Your Plans with Others

Sharing your thoughts with your advisor, department placement chair, and others who will work with you in your search can help these individuals act effectively on your behalf. Conversation with them can help you clarify your own thinking as it evolves. Honest faculty feedback about how realistic your choices are can be enormously helpful to you. The best way for you to elicit it is to ask for candor, assuring those you ask that your feelings will not be hurt by what you hear. Needless to say, respond in a way that does not cause someone to regret his or her candor.

In talking to others, whether faculty members or peers, keep your own priorities clearly in mind, and use your own judgment. Consider, for instance, your feelings about raising research funds. In some fields, such as the sciences and engineering, you must do so successfully and repeatedly to achieve tenure at a major research institution. If you have a realistic chance of obtaining a position at a major research institution, but privately feel that meeting the research demands necessary to get tenure there will consign you to years of prolonged misery, then it may be wise for you to look at another type of institution.

Perhaps your graduate work has only recently begun to take off because you were meeting personal obligations that you are now convinced will be lighter. In that case you may want to try for jobs that your advisor feels are beyond your reach, even if you need to take a postdoctoral position in the interim to strengthen your credentials. If you are a natural risk-taker convinced that a small but growing department may be the source of some of the most exciting work in your field, you may choose to ignore the cautions of more conservative friends who say, "Yes, but who's ever heard of it?"

Following your own instincts as to what you will find satisfying is easy if your goals are similar to those of the people around you. It is often more difficult if you want to follow a path that seems foreign to your advisor and most of the students in your department. In that case, use their skepticism as a prod to make sure that you get as much information as possible so that you make informed decisions. If you want to do something nontraditional, be able to explain your decision to others so they can support your search.

Balance this skepticism, however, with the enthusiasm of people who are doing what you would like to do, even if they are at other institutions and you have to seek them out. In the end, it is your career and your life, and you are most likely to be satisfied with both if you shape them according to your own priorities and values.

Chapter 5
The Importance of Advisors and Professional Networks

A job search may feel like a lonely enterprise, but it is always conducted within the context of a web of social relationships. You work within a discipline with its own language, conventions, and structure of communication. Your own research has undoubtedly been strengthened by communication with other people; in some fields it has been conducted as part of a team. You are leaving a department with one social structure and culture to enter another. You will be explicitly recommended by several people, and those who are considering your candidacy may hear about you from others.

Whether you find these facts reassuring or alarming, by taking account of them as early as possible in your graduate career, you can strengthen your prospects in the job market. If you have not paid sufficient attention to them until now, it is not too late to focus on them. Networking is crucial, not only to get a job, but also to succeed at it and at your research. Some candidates are put off by the potentially exploitative aspect of networking, as well they should be. The goal is not to use people in a one-way exchange, but to engage in a mutually beneficial relationship.

During graduate study it's critical that you change your self-concept from that of a "student" who primarily learns from others to that of a "colleague" who is actively engaged in his or her chosen discipline. If you view yourself merely as a job-hunting student, you will see networking as a petitionary activity, be hesitant to contact people, and perhaps run the risk of being bothersome. If you view yourself as an active member of your discipline, you will view networking more appropriately as an exchange of information, contact people confidently, and usually make them happy that they got to know you.

Advisors and Mentors

It is difficult to overemphasize the importance of an advisor in an academic career. When you enter the job market, and perhaps for years, you will often be viewed as "X's student," while your success is an important element in your advisor's professional reputation. In some fields, your postdoctoral supervisor is also extremely important. If your advisor or supervisor is well known in the market you want to enter, thinks highly of you, spends time with you, is savvy about the employment market, and is enthusiastically supportive of your job search, you will be likely to think highly of the importance of the advisor's role. Your first job search may well go more smoothly because you will be able to discuss your goals with your advisor, who will in turn perhaps make phone calls that will pave the way to interviews.

While such a situation is generally enviable, you may also need to make a particular effort to distinguish between your own goals and your mentor's goals for you, if you feel they differ. Making choices that are disappointing to the advisor will be particularly difficult. You also may rely too heavily on your advisor's intervention and fail to master job-hunting skills as thoroughly as does someone who gets less assistance. If you are blessed with such an advisor, make a particular effort to learn from that person how best to make efforts in your own behalf. If you are doing postdoctoral research, your current supervisor can play a role in your search similar to that of an advisor. However, in addition to supporting your career development, a postdoctoral supervisor is also often dependent on your work to complete research. It may not be realistic to expect that person to enthusiastically support you for a position which would take you away before you completed the time you'd committed to the postdoctoral position.

You may have a less-than-ideal advising relationship. Perhaps your advisor is not particularly well known, brilliant but unskilled at interacting with other people, so formal and distant that you are honestly unsure what he or she thinks about your work, or, in fact, disappointed in your work and not hesitant to tell you so. Whatever the characteristics of this real human being, you can probably improve the relationship, profit from the individual's greatest strengths, and, if necessary, find additional mentors.

If things are not going well between you and your advisor, your natural tendency may be to avoid talking with him or her. Resist this temptation! It is only through interaction that you can identify problems and attempt to address them. Arrange regular meetings to discuss your work, come well prepared for them, ask for as much feedback as you can get, take your advisor's suggestions, and make sure he or she sees that you have done so.

If you sense that your advisor is not happy with what you are doing, but is not telling you why, ask more directly for feedback. You may learn that in fact there is no problem, or you may identify an issue you can address. View the immediate problem as an opportunity to learn more about how to manage conflict successfully, since you will encounter it again and again throughout your career.

Even though advisors have considerable power, it is not unlimited. Most will respect you more if you think independently, respectfully express disagreement when it exists, present your ideas persuasively, and generally act as if you accept responsibility for your own career.

Most advisors act responsibly; a few abuse their power. The latter are most likely to victimize those who are unwilling to challenge inappropriate treatment. If you honestly believe you are being treated unfairly or inappropriately, begin by learning what the norms for acceptable behavior are. For example, your advisor may be crediting your work appropriately according to standards in your field while you may feel it is being "stolen." You can ask questions of other faculty members and graduate students, see whether your institution has formal policies and guidelines governing the relationship between advisors and students, consult publications of your professional association, and use library and Internet resources to understand how your experience fits into the general scheme of things. If you determine that you truly are being treated unfairly, it is usually better, although not risk-free, to seek fairer treatment, preferably with extreme deliberation and the guidance and support of a senior person who understands your department well.

Whatever your relationship with your advisor, it is helpful to have as many senior people as possible interested in your success. Take advantage of every opportunity to talk to and get to know other faculty members in your department. Ask them for opinions, perspective, and feedback in areas where you genuinely value their expertise. It is not necessary or desirable to think of this interaction in terms of flattery. Research enterprises flourish on the exchange of ideas. Don't hesitate to develop mentors at other institutions as well.

Your peers in the department offer another valuable source of perspective and lifelong contacts. Be realistic about the extent to which you will be competing with them in the job market; many candidates overestimate it. By and large, you have different strengths and interests. You will be far more successful if you exchange information and ideas with other students than if you avoid interaction for fear of somehow giving them a competitive edge. Beware, however, of becoming too involved in exchanging job-hunt horror stories. Every department has its share; some are apocryphal, and overindulgence in listening to and recounting them blurs your perspective.

The farther along you are in your academic career, the more important it is that you have established an independent network of colleagues and peers. If you are going on the market again several years after earning your final degree, some of your most important recommendations may come from outside your degree-granting department. However, if you've lost touch with faculty members there, before you begin a search is a good time to reconnect.

Professional Associations

Ideally, even in the early years of graduate study, you have begun to develop membership in professional networks that extend beyond your department and university. Whatever your field, there is at least one, if not several, scholarly or professional associations devoted to the exchange of ideas. Conferences, electronic discussion lists and newsgroups, publications, and local and regional meetings are the most common means of exchange. Because of the importance of these organizations, they will be referred to again and again throughout this handbook. If you don't know those that are important in your field, ask faculty members in your department.

Calls for papers are probably posted in your department, announced through print and electronic vehicles of your scholarly association, and listed in additional scholarly resources on the Internet. You can also consult the "Deadlines" section of *The Chronicle of Higher Education* for such notices. If you feel that publications in major journals or presentations at national conventions are slightly beyond your reach at this point, look for regional or local meetings of national organizations and respectable but less prestigious journals. Attend as many presentations as you can. In addition to learning and gaining ideas from the material presented, you can see how others present their work and form your own conclusions about the most effective way to communicate ideas.

Individual Contacts

If you are interested in the work of someone at another institution, whether you learn of it through a conference, a publication, or word of mouth, it is appropriate to approach that person, by phone, mail, or e-mail, for a further exchange of ideas. Share your comments; send a copy of a related paper or a reprint of an article you wrote. Ask questions. Suggest a meeting at a conference you both will be attending. It goes without saying that your comments and questions should be sincere and intelligent. Given that, however, by taking the initiative you greatly expand the range of intellectual resources upon which you can draw and develop a broad network of professional contacts with whom you can remain in touch throughout your career.

In between meetings, many electronic listservs and newsgroups function as ongoing professional forums with conversation similar to what may be found in the breaks between presentations at conferences. Your thoughtful participation in relevant groups gives you an opportunity to cause a large number of people to recognize your name in a positive way, not a bad thing when you consider that yours may be one of hundreds in a pile of applications.

As for years reputations have been made by work people publish, so can they be made or destroyed by communications posted to the Internet. The Internet is faster. Journal referees will prevent you from publishing anything that is libelous, outrageous, or just plain stupid. The Internet offers no such protection. When you communicate on the Net, consider that your potential audience is literally worldwide, that you reach it instantly, and that your communication is probably archived. Look yourself up on a powerful search engine to see what potential employers may already know about you. You may also have concern for not precipitously putting out work that you later plan to publish, given how easy it is to appropriate material from the Web. Include a copyright statement on all documents you post.

Observers of people's responses to electronic communication have frequently noted that it tends to flow across normal hierarchical boundaries. If you find even very senior individuals who actively contribute to electronic newsgroups or who are avid users of electronic mail, you may find this a comfortable way to communicate with them, particularly after you have taken the time to become familiar with their work.

You impoverish your own work if you do not take advantage of the multiplicity of forums for the exchange of ideas and of the personal give-and-take that turns a good piece of work into an excellent one. While you should not do so for this reason alone, as you establish your own network of communication, you also expand the range of people who are interested in your success in the job market.

Chapter 6
Conference Presentations and Networking

Conferences and conventions are a major means of scholarly communication. They also provide an opportunity to meet people who can hire you or refer you to others who can. By the time you are an advanced graduate student, if not before, you should begin to participate in these meetings, which are an important means of communication in your discipline. As you near the end of your graduate work and enter the job market, conferences begin to play a more formal role in your job search. They may offer a job placement service or give you an opportunity to gain favorable exposure through presenting a paper, and they always give you a way to network informally with others.

You should almost certainly plan to attend the national meeting of the major association in your field in the year you are on the job market. If you can arrange to give a paper or participate in a poster session, try to do so.

Presentations

Each field has its own style for the delivery of presentations. If you are delivering a conference paper for the first time, ask your department what to expect and how to be prepared for it. In addition, check with your professional association to see whether it provides guidelines that help you answer the following questions.

Mode of Delivery

- Do you sit or stand?
- Do you speak from notes or read a paper?

- Do you answer questions at a "poster session"?
- How formally are papers presented? Is any form of humor ever appropriate?
- How long will you have to speak?
- Will there be questions from the audience? Will there be a moderator?

Presentation Aids

- Should you prepare handouts?
- Should you use overhead transparencies or slides?
- How large should a poster be?
- Will you be able to project images from a computer? If so, will it have Internet access?

Practice your presentation before you offer it. If you can give a departmental seminar, so much the better, but, in any case, deliver the talk to an audience that will give you feedback. If you will use materials in your presentation, include them in your practice session so that you are thoroughly comfortable handling them. Ask your colleagues to question the vulnerable points in your thesis so that you can practice fielding them. As you practice, make sure to speak loudly enough to be heard, look at your audience, and speak rapidly enough to hold your audience's attention but slowly enough that they can understand you.

Your materials should look as professional as you can make them. Have plenty of white space so they are easy to read. Keep material away from the outer edges of transparencies so the audience can read them even if they slip out of place on the projector. Avoid using dark background colors on slides. They absorb the heat from the projector lamp and pop out of focus. Check to make sure that materials when projected are clear from a distance. Your campus almost certainly has individuals who are expert in graphic presentation. Seek them out and use their help. As presentation software has become widely available, standards for visual presentations have been rising.

On the other hand, don't let graphics overtake your message. Visual and oral presentations should reinforce each other. The point of both is to communicate clearly and well, while maintaining the interest of the audience. Your presentation style, orally or on the screen, should never get in the way of the information.

Networking

Conferences vary in size according to your field, but they always offer you an opportunity to meet more people in your discipline in one place than you can ever encounter elsewhere. Even if they are not hiring, they are a source of potential information about their institutions, their departments, and their research. They may share information or remember you when you later apply to their departments; they may be people you can later contact for information.

But how do you meet them? Here are some suggestions:

- Determine some goals for the conference in advance to help you plan your time. For instance, perhaps you wish to meet particular people, attend specific presentations or discussions, and seek feedback on a topic connected with your research.
- Find out which faculty members from your department will attend. If there is anyone to whom you would particularly like to be introduced, see if they can help you.
- Find out whether your department will give a party at the conference. If it will, be sure to attend. If not, see whether you can interest the department in arranging one.
- Give a presentation or poster session.
- Wear your nametag, and don't be shy about introducing yourself. Don't assume people will remember you.
- Attend sessions that interest you and talk with the speakers afterward, using your interest in their presentations as an icebreaker.
- Participate in smaller interest groups which may have meetings apart from presentations. Some organizations, for example, have active women's groups.
- If possible, take part in informal social gatherings attended by members of your department and faculty from other institutions.
- Much information gets exchanged at receptions and informal social gatherings. If you are comfortable joining a group you don't know and introducing yourself, by all means do so.
- Arrange brief meetings with someone whose work particularly interests you in advance of the conference, independent of a hiring context. Most fields are fairly small worlds, and having people know you is helpful, even if not immediately so.
- If there is a choice of hotels, stay in whichever is the main site for the conference. The central location will justify any extra expense because it will make it easier to meet people.
- Introduce people to each other when you have a chance.

It is appropriate to walk up even to well-established faculty or research-ers and introduce yourself. Few people consider this an imposition. In fact, both established and less well-known faculty find it very flattering when students introduce themselves and say, "I've looked forward to meeting you."

If you are shy, you may prefer to meet people in structured situations. Rather than letting yourself become nervous about meeting people, think about the links between your work and that of those you'd like to meet. If it helps, think of meeting new ideas, rather than new person-alities. If you are very outgoing, it may be easier to introduce yourself to strangers. In either case, remember that networking works only if you make a good impression! When you meet new people, your interest in their work, your work, and the field should dominate your conversation.

If you are seeking information, elicit it naturally in the course of con-versation. If people feel that your main interest is to pump them for job information, you would be better off not speaking with them in the first place. Avoid being overly pushy with or fawning over established re-searchers. Courtesy and consideration are good guidelines. People who are considering a candidate for a faculty position are looking not only for someone who is creative and smart and has a great future, but also for someone who is going to be a good colleague, that is, pleasant to have around and work with.

A conference mixes social and professional events and behaviors. As a job candidate, keep the professional aspect of the gathering foremost in your mind. There is the possibility that someone you approach may assume that your interest is social or romantic, rather than professional. This still is more likely to be a problem for women, but occasionally is problematic for men as well. Make sure that your manner and attire con-vey a professional interest. If you are in doubt whether this is clear to the other person, stick to public settings (meetings and restaurants rather than suites or rooms), don't drink too much yourself, and disengage your-self from anyone who does.

Participating in a professional network is a valuable activity that will help you, not only in your search for your first position, but throughout your career as well. From it come possibilities for collaborative efforts, invitations to submit papers, and professional stimulation. So it's worth-while to begin the process, whether it comes easily or with difficulty.

Chapter 7
Letters of Recommendation

At some point in the screening process for nearly every job, and frequently as part of your initial application, you will be asked to ensure that letters supporting your candidacy reach the hiring department. The number requested varies, but three is typical. Since letters require the cooperation of others, allow yourself plenty of time to obtain them.

Choosing Your Recommenders and Asking for Letters

The choice of recommenders is important and merits careful thought. Your dissertation advisor, of course, and anyone else with whom you have worked closely will be your first and second letter writers. In choosing additional recommenders find someone who can talk about your teaching as well as a senior researcher in your field. Most of your letters will probably be from your own department, but it is also acceptable to ask for letters from scholars outside your institution, if they are very familiar with your work.

Of course it is helpful to have a letter from someone who is widely known in your field, but do not ask people to write on your behalf unless they really know your work. If you are applying for postdocs or for positions at top research institutions, letters will primarily speak to your strength as a researcher.

If you are applying for jobs that emphasize teaching, you will probably see some ads that require "evidence of excellence in teaching." Faculty generally agree that letters from students you have taught are not convincing on their own. One way to respond to this type of request is to ask the recommender who knows your teaching best to write a letter addressing your teaching. Give this person copies of student evaluations of your teaching, if you have them. He or she can incorporate overall numeric standings (perhaps giving a context for them, such as the departmental and school average scores), quotes from students' comments, and his or her own assessment based on first-hand observation.

In some professional fields, such as business and architecture, a letter from a former employer or consulting client may be helpful, especially for a school that values interaction with practitioners.

Ask for letters as much in advance as possible. Faculty members receive many requests for them. Phrase your request in such a way that if some-one does not feel comfortable writing for you, he or she can gracefully decline. A tactful approach might be, "I'd appreciate a recommendation from you if you feel you know my work well enough to recommend me." If there is someone who must serve as a recommender, such as an advi-sor, about whose opinion of your work you are in doubt, you may want to ask that person to discuss with you frankly the types of institutions for which he or she can enthusiastically support your candidacy.

While you should never take for granted that someone will recommend you with enthusiasm, don't feel you are imposing on faculty by asking them to be recommenders. The success of its students in the job mar-ket is one of the ways by which a graduate department is evaluated, and advisors with highly successful students enhance their own reputations. Therefore, when someone can honestly write a strong recommendation for you, it's in that person's interest to do so.

Discuss your plans with those who agree to write for you. Recommen-dations are most effective when they describe you as well-suited to a par-ticular goal. If appropriate, remind the person who will recommend you of your work and experience. Provide him or her with your vita, a copy of a paper you wrote, a dissertation chapter, a statement of your research goals, or anything else that would be helpful.

Phone Calls

Sometimes a search committee, seeking what they feel will be a more can-did evaluation, will call one or more of your recommenders. This is par-ticularly likely to be the case when the recommender is known to some-one at the hiring institution. Since letters of recommendation are almost uniformly positive, a spontaneous enthusiastic response to a potential employer's phone call is very helpful to you.

On the other hand, if the person who is called is totally surprised that you are applying to the institution that is calling, the call probably does not help your case. Thus, it is very important to keep recommenders ap-prised of every step of your job search. You can ask them to reassure those who call about any aspects of your candidacy that you believe schools may find problematic. For example, if you are married to someone who is gen-

uinely willing to move to the location where you take a job, your recommender can reinforce your statement that this is true if an employer raises
the subject. (While such inquiries on the part of an employer are not
legal, they certainly can occur.)

Also be aware that people whose names you have not given as recommenders may be called or e-mailed "off the record" by someone on a
search committee. This is particularly likely to be the case if you've obviously worked closely with someone well known to a person in the hiring
department. So if there's someone with whom you've worked closely
whose name you are not giving as a reference, pay as much attention to
that relationship as you do to those with your official recommenders.

Handling Negative Evaluations

Unfortunately, sometimes the difficult situation arises in which someone
who would normally be expected to be supportive of your job search,
such as an advisor, is not. Perhaps he or she is disappointed by the goals
you have set, or believes they are unrealistic. Perhaps he or she genuinely
does not believe you are as strong as other advisees in the past and does
not want to compromise a reputation by giving you a recommendation
stronger than he or she believes you deserve. Perhaps the person is re-
taliating for your resistance to some form of harassment. Perhaps you are
merely the victim of hostility generated in another area of the person's
life.

Whatever the cause, this situation is always difficult. Most likely you
hear of it from someone else who reports to you what has been said in a
letter or conversation. Perhaps you feel (rightly or wrongly) that, where
you might expect to find support, you are encountering an obstacle. Several approaches are available to you, none totally risk-free, but all, on
balance, more likely to be productive than is suffering in silence.

Direct Conversation

If you are dealing with a reasonable person who honestly does not think
highly of your abilities, at least in relation to the arena in which you have
chosen to compete, direct conversation may be productive. For example,
you might begin by saying, "I know that you think I'm overreaching in
some of my applications. Could you give me examples of institutions for
which you could honestly be supportive of my candidacy?" It is helpful
for you to remind yourself that no one has an obligation to strongly recommend a candidate against his or her better judgment. Even if the person's assessment of you is incorrect, he or she does have the right to an
opinion.

Advice

If you can find a knowledgeable person of whom to ask advice, it can be very helpful. In choosing someone in whom to confide, consider that person's judgment, experience, and willingness to keep your communication confidential. Individuals outside your department may be particularly helpful in the latter regard. Counselors in university counseling offices and career centers have a professional obligation to keep conversations confidential. So do campus ombudsmen, affirmative action officers, and staff members of other organizations, such as women's centers, chartered to protect the interests of members of a particular group. However, only personal counselors are legally able to hold reports of sexual harassment in confidence.

While such professionals may make a good sounding board, they are unlikely to know enough about the personalities of people in your department to be able to give you very specific advice. Another faculty member in the department is in the best position to suggest how you may strengthen your position with whoever is obstructing your search or, on occasion, to tactfully intervene. Also consider your dean's office. Frequently, it is structured so that an associate dean is responsible for graduate education. A good associate dean is a great place to start when a student has a real problem with an advisor. He or she will know the personalities of the people in the department and the standards and dynamics of the school, and may be helpful if he or she also has a reputation for keeping conversations in confidence.

Intervention

The best antidote to a negative or lukewarm evaluation is a positive one. Those who strongly support your candidacy can write particularly enthusiastic letters or make phone calls on your behalf. Conceivably they can, if willing, suggest to hiring institutions that one of your key recommenders is misjudging you. However, be extremely careful about an offer to do this on your behalf. Often any attempt to contradict criticism merely strengthens the hiring committee's impression that there must be something behind the controversy.

It is usually safer for your advocates merely to express enthusiasm for your candidacy, leaving employers free to form their own conclusions. Recommendations from those outside your department who know your work can be particularly helpful in this regard, as they obviously represent a different perspective.

Campus Credentials Services

Your campus career center may offer you the valuable opportunity to keep a file of letters of recommendation which you can update easily and which are always immediately available. If it is the policy of your department to write new letters for each job a student applies for, you may want to have at least a backup file with the credentials service. Faculty go on sabbatical, get sick, or become extra busy and are not available to write customized letters for every job.

If you maintain a file of letters of recommendation, federal law gives you the option of maintaining nonconfidential letters to which you may have access. Generally these letters are not considered as credible as confidential ones.

Choosing the Recommendations to Send with an Application

Whatever you place on file, strengthen your presentation for a job by sending recommendations selectively. Even if your file contains many recommendations, don't send them all. Three or four strong letters are usually all you need. You may choose different subsets of recommendations depending upon the job's requirements.

Chapter 8
Learning About Openings

Once you have decided what kinds of jobs to pursue, there are several resources you can use to ensure that you learn about all the opportunities that might interest you.

Scholarly Associations

Every discipline has a scholarly association that serves its members in many ways. The association functions as the recorder and critic of scholarship in the discipline by producing one or more scholarly journals of refereed articles. It normally also holds a conference, usually on an annual basis, where the most recent research in the field is presented. There are many forms of conference presentation. Individual scholars, both Ph.D.s and advanced graduate students, present papers they have prepared for the conference; groups of scholars participate in panel discussions; and individuals or research teams participate in poster sessions or other small group discussions of their work. Such conferences or conventions provide an opportunity for formal and informal communication on research and are crucial for keeping the discipline dynamic. Scholarly associations also provide several job-related services.

Job Listings

Sometimes as part of a journal, but more often as a separate bulletin and on a Web site, most scholarly associations regularly publish a listing of postdoctoral and tenure-track academic job openings. When an academic department has an opening, it is customary to advertise the position in an association job bank, in print or online. The institution pays the association a fee to place the advertisement.

In many cases, the job listings are available to members only. However,

most associations offer membership to students at a reduced rate. Sometimes it is possible to subscribe to the job listings separately.

Your department probably receives the job listings from the corresponding association and possibly listings from related associations as
well. Find out which job opening publications your department receives
and where they are kept. Better still, get your own subscription. If it is not
normally sent first class, find out whether it can be for an extra fee. Also
find out whether the listings are available electronically. When there are
active electronic discussion lists in a field, jobs are often posted to them
as well.

Job Placement

Many scholarly associations provide some kind of job placement program
at their annual conventions. This can range from simply making interview rooms available to maintaining notebooks or computer printouts
of recent job openings to running formalized placement operations with
scheduled interviews for employers and candidates. Check with your association to see what kind of placement program it has. Of course, individual institutions also conduct interviews in their rooms or suites during
conventions (see Chapter 15, "Off-Site Interviews: Conference/Conven-
tion and Telephone Interviews").

Literature on Job Hunting

Some associations produce job hunting guides for their members. These
can range from a single sheet of interviewing techniques to a published
book covering all aspects of the job search in that field. Such guides often
cover nonacademic careers as well as academic employment.

Regional Associations

In addition to a regional chapter of your national association, you may
find additional relevant local and regional associations. These usually
have an annual meeting on a smaller scale and often offer some sort of
job placement. Check with your advisor about these.

If you do not know which association is appropriate for your field ask
your advisor and other faculty in your department, check the subject index of the latest issue of *National Trade and Professional Associations*, or
check Appendix 1 of this book.

National and Local Publications

The Chronicle of Higher Education, the national newspaper of higher education, lists teaching positions across the United States as well as some international ones. Most college and university libraries and campus career centers receive it. Its job listings are on the Internet *Chronicle* site at <www.chronicle.com/jobs> and, with the exception of the most recent week's, are available at no cost to readers. The Internet version is searchable. In the print version, job openings are listed in two ways: an alphabetical listing by job title; and display listings placed in no order, indexed by subject at the beginning of the section.

The bimonthly *Black Issues in Higher Education* is a newsmagazine dedicated exclusively to minority issues in higher education. It has an extensive job listing section.

Never to be used as the sole source of job listings, but useful to those seeking part-time teaching jobs or positions in small two-year colleges, is the local newspaper employment section. Positions in higher education are usually listed under "Education," and mixed in with educational administration and elementary and secondary teaching.

Institutional Web Sites

Increasingly, institutions are posting job openings to their own Web sites. This is particularly true of administrative positions. However, posting of faculty positions is rapidly increasing. While it isn't practical to search every institution in the country regularly, if you have a geographic preference or constraint, it may be practical to bookmark every institution in a given radius that posts its faculty openings to its Web site and to check these locations regularly. A quick way to find the employment menus of college and university Web sites is to go to *Jobs in Higher Education* at <www.academic360.com>. The site has links to lists of international institutions and community colleges, as well.

Your Network

Faculty in your department receive announcements from colleagues at other schools where there are openings. Keep a high profile in your department so that they will think of you when they hear about jobs. Know where your department posts jobs and check there regularly.

For temporary non-tenure-track jobs you may make direct inquiries of departments that interest you. This approach works best when you can give department chairs a rationale for your call, such as an interest in a particular kind of school or in schools in a clearly defined geographic area.

Additionally, keep in touch with everyone you know who might hear about openings: for example, former fellow graduate students who have already found jobs, former professors at other institutions, and people you have met at conferences. Let them know when you are beginning your job search and nearing the end of your dissertation. Be sure to thank anyone who notifies you of a job opening even if it doesn't work out or is not a good fit for you.

Part III
Written Materials for the Search: Suggestions and Samples

Chapter 9
Responding to Position Announcements

When you apply for any college or university teaching position, you will be asked to submit a "curriculum vitae," a "vita," or a "c.v." All these terms apply to the same document, which is a summary of your education, experience, publications, and other relevant data. In addition you may be asked for any or all of these: a dissertation abstract, a summary of your future research plans, a statement of your teaching philosophy, a chapter of your dissertation or an entire research paper, and "evidence of successful teaching." Members of the hiring committee may check your Web site, but a site is not generally required as part of an application. Some community colleges and state universities require that a completed application form accompany your other materials. Check to see whether a standard application is needed.

What is required varies from field to field. Check with your department to make sure that what you are sending is within the conventions of your field. Sometimes you may find that job announcements ask that you "send credentials" or "send dossier." These terms do not have a standard meaning. You can usually assume that what it is meant is a cover letter, a vita, and letters of recommendation. Sometimes a transcript is also required. Be guided by your department's advice about what is usual in your field. Probably the only way to be absolutely certain about what is desired by a given department that has used a vague phrase in its ad is to call and ask.

Sometimes application is a two-stage process, in which applicants initially send minimal information and some are further selected to send more detailed materials, such as a dissertation chapter or letters of recommendation. Use discretion in sending supporting materials that have not been requested. If you do, explain why you have in your cover letter.

Chapter 10
Vitas

Whether or not it is accompanied by letters of recommendation, your vita is always the first thing you will send to a hiring institution, whether it is called a "vita," a "c.v.," a "curriculum vitae," or, occasionally, a "resume." In preparing it, your goal is to create enough interest in your candidacy that you are granted a personal interview. Design your vita so that your strongest qualifications stand out if an employer skims it for only a few seconds, and with enough supporting detail so that it will stand up to scrutiny during a thorough reading.

Getting Started

Before beginning to write your vita, review your educational and professional history. Using the categories suggested below, list everything you imagine could possibly be included. Eventually you will decide what to include or exclude, but begin by ensuring that you are not overlooking anything relevant. Write a draft, experiment with the format, eliminate irrelevant information, have the vita critiqued, and make at least one more draft before you produce the final version.

Organization and Content

A vita always includes your name and contact information and information about your education, professional experience, publications, presentations, and honors. It may also include professional, extracurricular, and community activities; professional memberships; foreign languages; research interests; teaching competencies; grants; and selected personal data. Your name and information about how to contact you should appear at the top of the first page. If you are completing a Ph.D., the first section will be "Education." If you are applying from a postdoc or current faculty position, you may put your experience first. Follow with categories in decreasing order of importance. One exception is publications; if you have a long list, convention usually places it at the end of your vita. Within each category, give information in reverse chronological order, from most recent backward. Be concise; use phrases rather than complete sentences.

Name

Make sure that it appears on every page. After the first page, also include a page number.

Contact Information

Include both home and office addresses, e-mail, phone and fax numbers, and URL, if you have one. Use only phone numbers at which you are sure that messages will be delivered reliably. If you will be available at a number or address before or after a specific date, say so.

Objective

A vita for a faculty or postdoctoral position, in contrast to a resume for a nonacademic position, typically does not include an "Objective," or statement of the type of position you want. A possible exception is the unusual situation in which your goals are very different from what most employers would imagine from your vita.

Education

Discuss your graduate and undergraduate work in detail. List each institution, degree, field of concentration, and date at which a degree was received. Search committees want to know when your dissertation will be finished, so indicate the anticipated date of completion. If you are just beginning your dissertation and preparing a vita for a fellowship or part-time position, you may want to include a date for the latest formal stage of graduate work you have completed ("Coursework completed, May 2001"; "Passed examinations with distinction, May 2001"; or whatever formal marker of progress your program may have).

Always include the title of your dissertation and the name of your advisor. You may include the names of committee members if you think their inclusion will be helpful to you. You may also list additional research projects or additional areas of concentration. You may include activities related to your graduate training; for example, "President, Graduate Chemistry Society." If you have been very active in graduate student government, you may wish to create a separate section entitled "Committees," or "University Service," which would appear after listings of more relevant academic detail. Do not include high school. If you want to include it in case alumni will recognize it, mention it briefly in a personal section at the end.

Honors

Whether you make this a separate section or a category under "Education" depends on how important honors are in your qualifications. If you have received several prestigious and highly competitive awards, for example, you may highlight them in a separate section. On the other hand, if you have few honors, you probably do not want to call attention to that fact by creating a category with only one unimpressive entry.

Commonly known honors (Phi Beta Kappa) need no explanation, but other awards can be briefly explained. Foreign students, in particular, may want to stress the degree to which an unfamiliar award was competitive (for example, "One of three selected from among 2,000 graduating chemists nationally").

Experience

In this section, include all the experience that you now view as relevant to your professional objectives. For each position you have held, include the name of the institution with which you were associated, your responsibilities and accomplishments, dates, and, in most cases, your position title. Pick a format that you plan to use consistently. List positions or employers first in each entry depending on which format, on balance, shows you to best advantage. Sometimes a general heading of "Experience" will be appropriate, but frequently you will want to subdivide the section. A common division is "Teaching Experience" and "Research Experience."

Describe each item to give the reader an overview of what you did, together with details about the most interesting or impressive aspects of your position. Stress what you accomplished and uniquely contributed. Use verb phrases and make every word count. Thus "Responsibilities included developing various new course materials and instructional aids," becomes "Developed syllabus and diagnostic exam later adopted by department."

If you are describing a research project, give a brief introductory statement indicating what you set out to accomplish and what results you obtained. This is not, however, the place for a complete dissertation abstract.

Professional Experience

If you are applying for a position in a professional school and have experience working in that profession, describe it in some detail. If your professional experience is not related to your current scholarly pursuits, include it, but condense it drastically.

Licensure/Registration/Certification

List these credentials for positions in professional schools in fields where they are required, for example, nursing, education, architecture.

Publications/Presentations

Although these are of extreme importance for an academic position, convention usually places them last once they have grown beyond a few entries. They are listed in standard bibliographic form for your field. If you have a very long list, they may be subcategorized by topic or by publication format. Subcategorizing by topic is a good way to call attention to areas of expertise which may not be readily apparent. While it is acceptable to list articles as "submitted," or "in preparation," too many citations of this form not balanced by articles that are either published or in press can strike a pathetic note.

Be aware of prestige hierarchies, and don't dilute the credibility of presentations at established scholarly societies or articles in refereed journals by including term papers or publications in popular journals or newspapers. Separate refereed articles from everything else. Dissertations are not usually considered publications unless they are subsequently published in a journal or as a book by a recognized publisher. Don't pad your publications list and don't include in it anything you would not want a hiring committee to read.

Grants

If you have received funding, list the funding agency and the project(s) for which it was awarded. Candidates frequently list dollar amounts for major funded research projects. Usually you would list fellowship or dissertation support with "Honors." Occasionally a grant will appear in two sections of the vita. It may be listed briefly under "Honors," and the work it supported discussed in detail under "Experience."

Scholarly and Professional Memberships/Leadership

List memberships or committee work in scholarly or professional organizations. If you have been very active in university committee work, you might also include it here, or perhaps create a separate section to cover it. If you have organized or moderated conference sessions, this would be an appropriate place to say so.

Research Interests

This optional category gives a brief answer to the question: "What are your future research plans?" Interests listed here should be described at a level specific enough to be credible and general enough to indicate the direction your research might take over the next several years. You may also be asked to submit a brief (one or two page) discussion of your future research plans as a separate part of your application. Be prepared to discuss in detail anything that you put in this section.

Teaching Competencies

You may use this optional category if you feel that the areas you are qualified to teach are not entirely obvious from the rest of the entries in your vita. Its listings are more general than "Research Interests." Be careful not to list such a wide range of competencies that your list lacks credibility. If you list a subject as a teaching competency, some other part of the vita should reinforce your qualifications to teach it. Be prepared to discuss your ideas about a syllabus/text for any course you list in this section.

Additional Information

Sometimes called "Personal," this optional section may encompass miscellaneous information that does not fit elsewhere. You may include knowledge of foreign languages (if they are not very important to your research; if they are, you might give them their own section), extensive travel, and interests that you feel are important. If you worked prior to attending graduate school at jobs you now consider irrelevant, you may summarize them with a statement such as "Employment 1996–1998 included office and restaurant work." You need not include date of birth or a statement about your health. We recommend you do not include marital status unless you are sure it will work to your advantage to do so.

If anything in your vita may make an employer question whether you have United States work permission (for example, an undergraduate degree from another country), list U.S. citizenship or permanent residency if you have it. If you do not, either make the most positive statement you can about work eligibility, for example, "Visa status allows 18 months United States work permission," or omit any mention of citizenship.

References

List the people who write letters of recommendation for you and identify their institutions. Providing their telephone numbers and e-mail addresses is an added convenience to employers, if your recommenders are prepared for informal inquiries. Complete mailing addresses are not really necessary on the vita, because when written recommendations are required it is almost always your responsibility to see that they arrive. For this reason, the names of references are sometimes omitted on the vita.

Tailoring Your Vita to Its Audience

Your vita should always include basic information and the information you present should always be true. However, if you are applying for two distinct types of positions, or positions in different types of institutions and departments, you may wish to develop more than one version of your vita. Variations could include choosing headings to emphasize information of particular relevance to a situation (for example, including "Administrative Experience" for positions that involve both teaching and administrative components); giving details about additional areas of concentration more relevant to one field than another; and using different subsets of individuals to recommend you for different types of positions. Differences between versions of your vita are usually subtle, but can be effective nonetheless. Consider different versions if you are in an interdisciplinary field and will apply to more than one type of department.

If you plan to apply for nonacademic positions that are not research-based, you will need an entirely different version of your vita, which will be called a "resume." We have included a few examples of resumes prepared by Ph.D.s pursuing nonacademic positions. For more discussion and examples, see the excellent *Outside the Ivory Tower: A Guide for Academics Considering Alternative Careers*, by Margaret Newhouse. For scientists, *To Boldly Go: A Practical Career Guide for Scientists*, by Peter S. Fiske, is a good additional source.

Experienced Candidates

If you are several years past your first academic position, your vita will be longer than that of a new Ph.D. Its general appearance and construction, however, will be similar. Generally you will omit details about earlier experience, while retaining mention of the experience itself. For example, your first vita may have given detail about what you did as a teaching assistant. Now you may merely list the position, without discussion of responsibilities. Your education will probably continue to remain at the top of the first page, although the amount of detail you provide about it may diminish.

If entries in some of the categories in your vita are growing numerous, you may begin to introduce subdivisions. For example, publications may be divided among books, papers, and reviews. Your listings of professional associations may begin to include discussions of conference sessions that you moderated or organized.

Length

How long a vita may be varies from field to field. Check with your department. In any case, be as concise as possible. Many graduate students will be able to manage with not more than two pages, including publications. Naturally, the vitas of more experienced candidates will be longer.

Layout and Reproduction

Remember that you are designing your vita to capture your readers' attention at a first glance. Therefore pay attention to where you put information and how you format it. Organize the first page so that it contains the information about your greatest assets. That way the reader will be motivated to turn the page! Longer entries will call more attention to themselves than will shorter ones. Material near the top of the page will stand out more than that at the bottom. The left-hand column usually gets the greatest visual emphasis, so don't waste it on dates. Put dates on the right-hand margin, and use the left-hand margin for content items, such as names of institutions.

Take advantage of bold type for emphasis and establish a consistent graphic hierarchy so that typeface for equivalent categories of information is the same. An example of one typical hierarchy appears below:

HEADING (for example, **EXPERIENCE**)
Important Item (for example, **University of Excellence**)
Less Important Item (for example, *Teaching Assistant*)

Use one, or at the most, two, conservative fonts. Fonts smaller than 10 point are very difficult to read. Given the availability of bold and italic type, there's no need to clutter the page with underlining. Avoid the graphic dizziness caused by introducing too many kinds of type or indentations.

Proofread your vita again and again. If it contains typographical or spelling errors, it can cause you to be dropped from consideration. To be doubly sure, ask a friend who is a good proofreader to read the draft also. Use a laser printer for the original copy of your vita. Print it on office-quality paper (and, of course, single-sided). Have copies made by a printing service or generate multiple copies on a laser printer. Paper may be white, cream, or any other very conservative tint. Do not staple pages together, but make sure your name and a page number appear on each page.

Help

Because a vita is often the first thing an employer sees of you, it is too important a document not to be thoroughly critiqued and revised. Show it to your advisor and others in your department. If your campus career service has counselors who work with graduate students, they will also be glad to provide critiques and help you get your first draft together. To give your vita a good final test, show it briefly to someone who has not seen it and ask that person what he or she notices and remembers. If the most important items stand out, you're in good shape. Otherwise, more revision is order.

A Note About the Sample Vitas That Follow

The following examples, generously volunteered by real candidates, are provided to give you an idea of what such materials look like. Other than omitting the names of the authors, their advisors, committee members, coauthors, and institutions, and changing some dates, we have tried to alter them as little as possible. The examples are arranged by field: humanities, social sciences, science/engineering, and professional disciplines.

These examples should be regarded as excellent, but not necessarily perfect. They are not all in the same format, and they do not all subscribe to the same stylistic conventions, so you can see there are many ways to construct a good vita. The custom in your own field, or an unusual combination of strengths in your background, might well dictate that your vita should be quite different in style, language, or appearance. Don't attempt to copy any single example. Rather, look at all of them to see which forms of presentation might suit your own taste or situation.

Sample Humanities Vita
Web-based. Linked items are underlined.

EMILY CANDIDATE

E-mail Address

[Note: This candidate, like many posting a vita to the Web, has chosen not to include a phone number or mailing address.]

RESEARCH INTERESTS

Prosody, Discourse, Dialog, Integration of natural language processing and speech, Parsing, TAG, Cross-linguistic comparison of prosodic and/or discourse phenomena, Use of phonetic/phonological information in speech technology, Use of empirical data in linguistic research.

EDUCATION

University of X
  Department of Linguistics, **Ph.D.**, May 1998
  Dissertation: "The Interpretation and Realization of Focus: An Experimental Investigation of Focus in English and Hungarian"
  Advisor: Dr. Name
  Department of Computer and Information Science, **M.S.E.**, 1991
  Advisor: Dr. Name

Northwestern University
  Department of Linguistics, March 1986 - August 1988

University of California at Davis
  Linguistics Program, A.B. with honors, 1981

EXPERIENCE

Research Assistant, University of X, Summer 1989 - present
  XTAG Project: Linguistic analysis and grammar implementation for Wide coverage English Grammar; recruiting and training linguists for project; supervising implementation and debugging of massive grammar expansion; writing emacs macros, shell and perl scripts for large-scale or global grammar changes; scripting, narrating and organizing production of project video; preparation of detailed technical report on project.
  Supervisor: Dr. Name

Teaching Assistant, Introductory Linguistics, University of X, Spring 1991
  Supervisor: Dr. Name, Department of Linguistics

Instructor, Introductory Linguistics, University of X, Summer 1990

Teaching Assistant, Introductory Linguistics, Northwestern University, Fall 1987- Spring 1988
  Supervisors: Dr. Name & Dr. Name, Department of Linguistics

Research Assistant Northwestern University, Summer 1986 - Spring 1988
  Pilot study of librarians' question answering strategies, data to be used as basis for a reference librarian expert system.
  Supervisor: Dr. Name, Departments of Linguistics and Computer Science

HONORS and AWARDS

William Penn Graduate Fellowship, University of X, 1988 - 1992; Linguistics Institute Fellowship, 1991 and 1987; Presidential Fellowship, Northwestern University, 1986 - 1987; Phi Beta Kappa, University of California at Davis, 1981; Linguistics Citation, University of California at Davis, 1981

Emily Candidate, p. 2

PUBLICATIONS

"Determining Determiner Sequencing: A Syntactic Analysis for English," with Name. To appear in a forthcoming CSLI volume on Tree Adjoining Grammar, eds. Name and Name.
"Evolution of the XTAG System," with Name, Name, Name, and Name, To appear in a forthcoming CSLI volume on Tree Adjoining Grammar, eds. Name and Name.
[Eleven additional publications follow.]

INVITED TALKS

"The Interpretation and Realization of Focus: An Experimental Investigation." Talk given at Bell Labs, Lucent Technologies, July 1998.
"Linguistic Analysis as a Resource for NLP: Development and Exploitation." Talk given at Sun Microsystems Laboratories, January 1998.
[Two additional talks follow.]

PRESENTATIONS

"An Approach to Robust Partial Parsing and Evaluation Metrics," with Name, Name, and Name. Workshop on Robust Parsing, ESSLLI'96, Prague, Czech Republic, August 1996.
"Prosody and the Interpretation of Cue Phrases." IRCS Workshop on Prosody in Natural Language, University of X, August 1992. Proceedings: IRCS report no. 92 - 37.
[Two additional presentations follow.]

COMPUTER LANGUAGES and SOFTWARE

PERL, SHELL (C & Bourne), UNIX, LISP, PROLOG, XWAVES (Entropic), TCL, S, FRAMEMAKER, HYPERCARD

NATURAL LANGUAGES

English - native speaker
Spanish - written and spoken competence
Japanese - non-technical conversational ability
German - reading knowledge
Hungarian - familiarity as object of research

PROFESSIONAL ACTIVITIES

Reviewer, Language and Speech
Member, Linguistic Society of America
Member, Association for Computational Linguistics
[Three additional activities follow.]

MISCELLANEOUS

Employment 1982-1986: Psychiatric Research Technician, paralegal positions
Other interests: Travel, dogs, white water rafting, caves, fencing

Sample Humanities Vita

ELLEN SCHOLAR

Work Address   Home Address
URL   Home Phone
Work Phone   E-mail

EDUCATION

X University, Washington, DC
Ph.D., English, May 1998
Neoclassical Rhetoric, History of Rhetoric, Rhetorical Theory
Dissertation: John Quincy Adams and the Rhetoric of the Smithsonian's Inception
Advisor: Advisor's Name, Ph.D.
M.A., English, 1992, 19th-century American Literature

University of St. Thomas, Houston, TX
B.A., English, 1990, summa cum laude
Editor of literary magazine, President of International English Honor Society

PROFESSIONAL POSITIONS

Visiting Assistant Professor, United States Naval Academy, Annapolis, MD, Fall 1997-present

Instructor/Teaching Assistant, University of X, Washington, DC, Fall 1994 -Spring 1997

PUBLICATIONS

Increase and Diffusion of Knowledge: The Rhetorics of Science and Education in the Smithsonian's Inception, forthcoming (fall) in *Rhetoric Review*.

John Quincy Adams's Promotion of Astronomy and His Neoclassical Rhetoric, under second revision for publication in *ISIS*.
[Two additional publications follow.]

PAPERS AND PRESENTATIONS

John Quincy Adams's Neoclassical Rhetoric and His Arguments for the Advancement of Astronomy. American Society for the History of Rhetoric, with Eastern Communication Association, Baltimore, April 1997.

Combining Rhetoric and Stylistics: an Analysis of Persuasion in John Quincy Adams's Smithsonian Rhetoric. College English Association National Conference, Baltimore, April 1997.
[Two additional presentations follow.]

WORK IN PROGRESS

Critical edition of important speeches by Adams for Greenwood Press, to be co-authored with Prof. Name (University of Y)

Monograph based on my dissertation (John Quincy Adams and the Smithsonian's Founding Rhetoric)

E. Scholar, p. 2

COURSES TAUGHT

U.S. Naval Academy
>   America's Literary Coming of Age: 1860-1920
>   Rhetoric and Introduction to Literature (essays, stories, drama)
>   Rhetoric and Introduction to Literature (novels, poetry)

X University
>   Argumentative Writing (used networked computers)
>   Signs and Symbols in American Life
>   Rhetoric and Composition (networked computers)
>   Freshman Seminar, Literature and Writing (basic writing)
>   Advanced ESL/Business Writing (to clergy, including the Archbishop of Moscow)

Montgomery College, MD
>   Freshman Writing (with workshop)

PROFESSIONAL WRITING EXPERIENCE

Editorial Assistant, Smithsonian Institution, Washington, DC, 1990-1994

Recruiting Writer, University of St. Thomas, Office of Admissions, Houston, TX, 1989-1990

COMMITTEE AND SERVICE WORK

Freshman (Plebe) Curriculum Committee, May 1999-present

Integrity Development Seminar Facilitator: Volunteer to lead discussions in Naval Academy program for education in moral reasoning. Theme: "The Officer as Citizen." Scheduled two admirals as guest speakers. Fall 1998-present

Workshop and Brown Bag Lunch Coordinator: Organized hands-on workshops for writing instructors; arranged expert speakers. Edited newsletter on practical classroom ideas. 1997-1998

Editor Student Writing Handbook: Initiated handbook project for composition students. 1997-1998
[Five additional items follow.]

PROFESSIONAL ASSOCIATIONS

International Society for the History of Rhetoric
American Society for the History of Rhetoric
[Three additional memberships follow.]

LANGUAGES

Reading knowledge of: Ancient Greek, Latin, Italian, German, and Spanish

REFERENCES (sent separately)
[Names and institutions of five references follow.]

Sample Humanities Vita
Vita incorporates related nonacademic experience.

A. S. Candidate

Department Address

Home Address
Home Phone
Email

EDUCATION

University of X
Ph.D., Department of Romance Languages, Spanish, 1998
    Field exams: Medieval, Colonial, 19th and 20th-Century Latin American literature, Narrative genre
    Dissertation: *Delinquency and Detection in the Neopoliciaco Novel of Cuba and Mexico, 1972-97*
    Director: Advisor's Name
M.A., Department of Romance Languages, Spanish, August 1995

Barnard College, New York, NY
B.A., Political Science, 1985. Senior thesis: *Image-makers in the Koch-Cuomo Mayoral Campaign*

SCHOLARSHIPS, AWARDS & HONORS

Andrew W. Mellon Dissertation Fellowship, 1997-1998
University Research Fellowship, Faculty of Arts and Sciences, University of X, 1996-1997
Dissertation Fellowship, Summer 1996
Assistant to the Editors, Hispanic Review, University of X, 1994-present
Research Assistant to Professor Name, 1994-1995. Researched and edited his *Historia de la literature*
    hispanoamericana, volumes I and II.

TEACHING AND RELATED EXPERIENCE

Department of Romance Languages, University of X
Substitute Instructor, Spanish 202 (advanced Spanish reading and conversation), Fall 1997
Placement Advisor for French and Spanish, Fall 1997
Instructor, required language courses. Prepared syllabi, assignments and exams, graded students.
    Spanish 140 (fourth-semester Spanish), Summer 1997
    Spanish 120 (second-semester Spanish), Spring 1996
    Spanish 110 (first-semester Spanish) Fall, 1995
ACTFL Oral Proficiency Interviews in Spanish, all levels, 1995-present
Private tutor, beginning through advanced Spanish, 1996-present

Encyclopedia Britannica
Educational Software Consultant, Fall 1997. Consult on development directions for Web and multimedia-based
foreign language learning software.

Linguistic Data Consortium, University of X
Software Evaluator, Summer 1997. Directed evaluation team for foreign language teaching software.
    Developed evaluation criteria adopted by LDC; research possible in-house development of multimedia foreign
    language teaching programs.
Web Designer, Spring 1997. Designed *Con/Textos* Web site, a multimedia reading program for advanced students
    of Spanish, using short stories by García Márquez, Fuentes, Rulfo, Cortázar, Monterroso, and Ferre. Edited
    Monterroso story, providing background, activities, and interactive glossary.

Graduate School of Fine Arts, University of X
Computer Application Seminars, 1989-94. Taught faculty and staff computer and Internet applications.

A. S. Candidate, p. 2

CONFERENCES/LECTURES

"Género, subgénero 7 nation: la novela policiaca cubana." To be presented at the NEMLA annual convention in Baltimore, April 17-18, 1998.

"The novela negra and the neopoliciaco: Popular culture, mayhem and cultural dislocation." Presented in absentia at *Hispanics and the U.S.: An Interdisciplinary Conference*, University of San Francisco, October 1997. [Citations of five additional lectures follow.]

PUBLICATIONS

"Machismo, travestismo y revolución en dos novelas policiacas cubanas." Forthcoming in proceedings of IV Jornada Metropolitanas de Estudios Culturales, Summer 1998.

"Violence and Patriotism: *La novela negra* from Chester Himes to Paco Ignacio Taibo II.*" Journal of American Culture*, Fall 1997. [Citations of four additional publications follow.]

TEACHING AND RESEARCH INTERESTS

Spanish language, all levels
Latin American literature, colonial through present
Twentieth-century Latin American literature
Possible seminar topics: Identity and distortion in the Caribbean essay, Latino/a literature, poetry of the
    Vanguardia, gender and genre in the regionalist novel, literature of the *crack,* the Revolution in
    Mexican letters, Latin American detective stories
    Topics of interest: Gender, identity, nationalism, genre fiction

TRAVEL AND RESEARCH

Cemanahuac Educational Community, Cuernavaca, Mexico, Summer 1993. Intensive summer study in language, Mexican culture, anthropology, and history.
Oaxaca, Mexico, Summer 1994. Summer study in Mexican culture, and anthropology.
La Habana and Pinar del Rio, Cuba, May 1997. Dissertation research.

ACADEMIC SERVICE

Faculty-Student liaison for Spanish Graduate Group, Graduate Romanic Association, University of X
    Department of Romance Languages, 1997-1998.
Conference Co-Director and head of Spanish reading committee, Third Annual Graduate Student Colloquium,
    University of X, 1997.

REFERENCES

[Names, e-mail, and phone numbers of three references follow.]

Sample Social Science Vita

SHAWNA SCHOLAR
Address
Phone, Email

EDUCATION

Ph.D. in Sociology, **University of X** , 2000
Master of Arts in Sociology, 1996
Bachelor of Arts with Honors in Sociology, **Brown University**, 1993

DISSERTATION

'Jumpin' the Broom: Ethnicity and Identity after Intermarriage among Haitians in Boston (Name and Name, co-chairs)

AREAS OF SPECIALIZATION

Racial and Ethnic Relations
American Immigration
Qualitative Research Methods
Caribbean Immigrants in the United States

OTHER TEACHING AND RESEARCH INTERESTS

International Perspectives on Race
Sociological Dimensions of Racial and Ethnic Identity
Pedagogy and Related Issues in Teaching Sociology

ACADEMIC POSITIONS

Visiting Research Fellow, 1998-1999
Institute on Race and Social Division, Boston University

Visiting Instructor, Summer 1999, Spring 2000
Department of Sociology, Boston University

AWARDS AND FELLOWSHIPS

Dissertation Fellowship 1999 - **University of X, Center for African and Afro-American Studies**
Summer Dissertation Workshop Fellowship 1997 - **Social Science Research Council, International Migration Program**
ICPSR Summer Institute Award 1995 - **University of X, Institute for Social Research**
[Five additional awards follow.]

RESEARCH GRANTS

Doctoral Dissertation Grant 1999 - **Department of Sociology, University of X**
Henry A. Murray Dissertation Award 1998 - **Murray Research Center, Radcliffe College**
[Three additional grants follow.]

S. Scholar, 2

RESEARCH EXPERIENCE

Research Assistant

Harvard University, Graduate School of Education
Harvard Immigration Project
Interviews with recent Haitian immigrants in Boston; ethnographic observations in classrooms.
Project Directors: Name and Name

University of X, Department of Sociology
Survey of Black Doctorates in the Academic and Non-Academic Workplace
Preparation and distribution of mail questionnaire. Qualitative interviews with Black scholars.
Project Directors: Name and Name
[Five additional experiences follow.]

TEACHING EXPERIENCE

Instructor

Boston University, Department of Sociology, Summer, 1999
Course title: Introduction to Race, Ethnic and Minority Relations

University of X, Center for African and Afro-American Studies, Summer, 1997
Course title: Qualitative Research Methods with Professor Name

Graduate Student Instructor

University of X, Department of Sociology, Winter, 1997
Course title: Introduction to Sociology: Perspectives in Society, with Professor Name
Course title: Introduction to Sociology through Race Relations, with Professor Name
[Additional teaching assistant experience follows.]

PUBLICATIONS

"Caribbean Immigrants and the Sociology of Race and Ethnicity: Limits of the Assimilation Perspective," in
African-American Research Perspectives, vol. 4, no. 1 (Spring 1998)
[Two additional citations follow.]

PAPER PRESENTATIONS/WORKS IN PROGRESS

Name (Co-author), "Disaporic Haitian Identity: Reconceptualizing Post-Immigrant Identify Formation."
(Under review.)

PROFESSIONAL ACTIVITIES AND SERVICE

Discussant, 1999 Eastern Sociological Society Annual Conference, Boston, MA
Panel Organizer, 1998 Annual Conference of the Haitian Studies Association, Port-au-Prince, Haiti
Conference Organizer, 1998 Sociology Graduate Students Conference, University of Michigan
[Seven additional activities follow.]

COMMUNITY SERVICE

Diversity Training Facilitator, University of X, Ann Arbor MI
[Three additional activities follow.]

[Sections for **PROFESSIONAL ASSOCIATION MEMBERSHIPS** and **REFERENCES** follow.]

Sample Social Science Vita
Candidate holds a nonfaculty research position.

Shastri Researcher, Ph.D.
Work Address
Work Phone, E-mail

EDUCATION

UNIVERSITY OF X   Philadelphia, PA
Doctorate in Sociology   1995
Doctoral thesis: "Do As I Say, Not As I Do: Dilemmas in Child Abuse Prevention."
Awarded the Baltzell Prize for Outstanding Sociology Dissertation
Fellow, Department of Sociology

BRYN MAWR COLLEGE   Bryn Mawr, PA
MA in Sociology   1989
Master's thesis: "Problems in Intervention: The Crisis of Teenage Pregnancy."
BA in Sociology, with honors   1988
Honor's thesis: "The Scarlet 'A': A Sociopolitical Analysis of the AIDS Controversy in the United States."

PROFESSIONAL EXPERIENCE

Current Research

UNIVERSITY OF CALIFORNIA, LOS ANGELES   Los Angeles, CA
DEPT. OF PSYCHIATRY AND BIOBEHAVIORAL SCIENCES   1996–present
Assistant Research Sociologist (1998–present); Staff Research Associate (1996–1998)

Activities include project research, data analysis, paper and proposal writing, methodology instruction, and student mentoring/research oversight.

Youth to Adult Transitions in Three African Descended Groups (Name and Name, Key Investigators). Project in research program entitled The Community Adaptation of Mildly Retarded Persons (Name and Name, Principal Investigators). National Institute of Child Health and Human Development.
*   Director of Field Research for a longitudinal ethnographic study following the passage to adulthood of urban Black adolescents from three different African descended groups. This project observes and analyzes the transition experiences of Black youth from low and moderate income families and the extent to which they vary by gender, ethnic identity, personal efficacy, and social context.

Mate Availability, Family Formation and Well-being: The Study of Families and Relationships (Name and Name, Principal Investigators). National Institute of Mental Health.
*   A 21-city survey project examining the relationships between family formation, life and marital satisfaction, and mental health as well as the community level contextual influences on these variables.
[One additional project follows.]

Previous Research

THE EVALUATION AND TRAINING INSTITUTE   Los Angeles, CA
Project Manager   1995–1996
Engaged in a range of activities for a consulting firm including writing project proposals and reports; evaluating social and educational policy programs; moderating focus groups and committees; performing qualitative research through interviews, observations, and content analysis; making client presentations; and developing project budgets.

NATIONAL COMMITTEE TO PREVENT CHILD ABUSE   Chicago, IL
Research Associate with Dr. Name   1992–1994
Investigated the effect of prevention programs on the child rearing and disciplining behavior of specific populations. Funded by the William Penn Foundation. Responsible for evaluations at sites in the metro Philadelphia area; interviews conducted in English and Spanish.

UNIVERSITY OF X   Philadelphia, PA
Research Associate with Professor Name   1993–1994
Analyzed the professional networks of top CEOs, directors, and money managers and the corresponding impact on American business culture.
[Three additional research experiences follow.]

University Teaching

UNIVERSITY OF CALIFORNIA, LOS ANGELES   Los Angeles, CA
Women's Studies Program   1999
Visiting Assistant Professor: Women and Health Care in the U.S.

MT. ST. MARY'S COLLEGE   Los Angeles, CA
Department of Sociology   1997–present
Lecturer: Multicultural and Multiethnic Issues for Health Care Professionals (3 terms), Research Methods and Social Statistics, and Deviant Behavior: Juvenile Delinquency

UNIVERSITY OF PENNSYLVANIA   Philadelphia, PA
College of General Studies   1993–1995
Instructor: Field Methods of Social Research (2 semesters), Deviance and Social Control, and Introduction to Sociology

Graduate Program of City and Regional Planning   1994
Lecturer: Social Stratification and the Future of Cities

Department of Sociology   1990–1993
Teaching Assistant: American Society, Introductory Sociology (2 semesters), Deviance and Social Control (2 semesters), and Corporations and Managers

ST. JOSEPH'S UNIVERSITY   Philadelphia, PA
Department of Sociology   1994
Instructor, Social Deviance

PAPERS/PUBLICATIONS

Candidate's Name (1999). "When Prevention Fails: The Role of Context in Persistent Child Abuse." Under review.

Candidate's Name; Name & Name (1999). "Can't Buy Me Love? Economic Considerations in Mate Selection Criteria." Under review.
[Five additional publications follow.]

PRESENTATIONS

University of California, Los Angeles, April, 1999. Psychiatry M210/Anthro M234: Seminar in Psychocultural Studies and Medical Anthropology.

Shastri Researcher, p. 3

University of California, Los Angeles, February, 1999. Psychiatry 238: The Use of Survey Research Techniques in Psychocultural Studies. "The Processing of Qualitative Data."

Caribbean Studies Association, May, 1998. "Disparities between Immigration Expectations and Outcomes: Experiences of Garifuna and Belizean Parents in Los Angeles." Presented at the annual meeting in Antigua. [Nine additional presentations follow.]

CONTINUING EDUCATION

Research Participant, Family Research Consortium III, Summer Institute. Bretton Woods, NH; June, 1999

University of California, Los Angeles: Qualitative Data Analysis Software Workshop. April, 1999

University of California, Los Angeles, Writer's Program: Writing and Publishing the Academic Article. Winter 1999
[Two additional sessions follow.]

COMMITTEE SERVICE

Society for the Study of Social Problems
Minority Scholarship Committee

University of California, Los Angeles
Multimethod Taskforce
Westchester High School Healthy Start Collaborative Outreach Project

University of X
University Academic Planning and Budget Committee, Committee on Academic Integrity for the Judicial Inquiry Office, Graduate Sociology Admissions Committee, and Sociology Graduate Student Representative

Bryn Mawr College
Southern California Alumnae Career Development Coordinator, Reunion Gift Committee, Student Representative Council Co-President, Dorm President, Hall Advisor, First Year Orientation Leader, Admissions Committee, Sociology Majors' Representative, and Independent Majors' Committee

MEMBERSHIPS

The American Sociological Association, Society for Applied Sociology, Society for the Study of Social Problems, Caribbean Studies Association, Sociologists for Women in Society, American Association of University Professors, and the Pacific Sociological Association

FOREIGN LANGUAGES

Strong reading, writing, and speaking ability in Spanish; speaking and reading ability in French.

Sample Social Science Vita

ELENA SCHOLAR
Address
Work Phone
Home Phone; E-Mail

EDUCATION

Ph.D. in Anthropology, University of X, May 2000
Dissertation: The Organization of Late Classic Lithic Production at the Prehistoric Maya Site of Colha, Belize:
    A Study in Complexity and Heterarchy
Advisor: Dr. Name
Areas of Interest: the Americas, focusing on Mesoamerica; complex societies; rainforest ecology; history of
    anthropology; public education and preservation of the past
School of Arts and Sciences Dissertation Fellow, 1988
National Science Foundation Graduate Fellow, 1978-81

Archival Certification, Academy of Certified Archivists, Chicago, IL, 1991
Tower Fellow, Ecole Normale Superieure, Paris, France, 1977-78
B.A., Radcliffe College, Harvard University, Cambridge, MA, 1977
    magna cum laude with highest honors in Anthropology

GRANTS

Department of Anthropology, University of X, 1981, 1983, 1987, 1988
Department of Anthropology, University of Arizona, 1980
Department of Anthropology, Harvard University, 1976
Radcliffe Union of Students, Radcliffe College, Harvard University, 1976

Languages: native fluency in French, fluent in Spanish

ARCHAEOLOGICAL FIELDWORK

Colha Project, Colha, Belize, Directors: Name and Name
    Consultant, 1994
    Field Director, 1987
    Co-Field Director, 1986
[Fourteen other fieldwork entries follow.]

UNIVERSITY TEACHING EXPERIENCE

Credit Courses

Department of Anthropology, University of X, Philadelphia, PA
    Lecturer: The Ancient Maya, Fall 1991
    Upper-level undergraduate course providing an overview of Maya culture history while examining such issues
    as the origins and demise of Classic civilization. Also included an in-depth look at political, economic, and
    social organization, iconographic and writing systems, and the relationships between architecture, art, artifacts,
    and belief systems.
[Three additional teaching experiences follow.]

Non-Credit Courses

Commonwealth of Pennsylvania Museum Outreach Program, The University Museum, Philadelphia, PA
    Program offers selected lectures to libraries, community centers, and other public venues on an occasional basis.
    Lecturer, 1984-present. Lectures on the Maya, the Amazon, history of anthropology, and archives.

Elena Scholar, 2

School of Continuing Studies, Johns Hopkins University, Baltimore, MD. School offers short weekly evening lecture series for interested adults.
Lecturer, "The Forgotten World of the Ancient Maya," Fall 1993. Organized course and gave two of six lectures, on new discoveries in archaeology and epigraphy and on daily life and subsistence.
[One additional entry follows, listing nine short courses.]

PROFESSIONAL EXPERIENCE: ARCHIVES

College Archivist, Gwynedd-Mercy College, Gwynedd Valley, PA, 1991-present

Archival Consultant, Institut fur Geschichte und Theorie der Architektur (GTA Eidgenossische Technische Hochschule (ETH) - Honggerberg, Zurich, Fall 1992
[Four additional archival positions follow.]

PROFESSIONAL EXPERIENCE: MUSEUMS

Exhibit Consultant, American Section and Education Department, the University Museum, Philadelphia, PA, 1990. Wrote teacher's guide for the exhibit "The Gift of Birds: Featherwork of Native South American Peoples."

Grant Writer, American Section, the University Museum, Philadelphia, PA, 1989. Wrote implementation grant for the exhibit "The Gift of Birds: Featherwork of Native South American Peoples."
[Five other positions are listed.]

PROFESSIONAL SERVICE

Member, Delaware Valley Archivists Group Planning Committee, 1996-present
Volunteer Consultant and Instructor for Project Archaeology, Doylestown Public Schools and Fonthill Museum, 1996-98
Member, Society for American Archaeology Committee on the History of Archaeology, 1989-present
Board Member, University City Arts League, 1993-96. Chair, Personnel Committee
Chair, symposium on Certification and Recertification: 5 Years After, Mid-Atlantic Regional Archives Conference, Fall 1995
[Three additional professional activities follow.]

PUBLICATIONS

In press. Farabee, William Curtis. *Dictionary of American National Biography*, Oxford University Press.

1996 The Archival Management of Archaeological Records. *The Oxford Companion to Archaeology*, Brian M. Fagan (ed. in chief), Charlotte Beck, George Michaels, Chris Scarre, and Neil Asher Silberman, eds., pp. 45-46. New York, NY: Oxford University Press.
[Six other citations follow.]

PAPERS

1998 "Project Archaeology, Pennsylvania Style." To be presented at the symposium Anthropology and the Three R's: Reaching the Next Generation, organized by Name and Name for the 97th annual meeting of the American Anthropological Association, Philadelphia, PA, December 5. (Senior author with Name.)
[Thirteen additional citations follow.]

POSTER SESSIONS

1990 "Tool Production Strategies at Colha, Belize." Presented at the 55th Annual Meeting of the Society for American Archaeology, Las Vegas, NV, April 21. (Junior author with Name.)

Sample Science Vita

ERIC RESEARCHER

Work Address
Phone
Email
US citizenship

EDUCATION

University of X, Ph.D., Biology, May 1993

Swarthmore College, Swarthmore, Pennsylvania, B.A., May 1986. Major: Biology

Collège Cardinal Mercier, Brainé L'Alleud, Belgium. Maturité, July 1982

PROFESSIONAL EXPERIENCE

California Institute of Technology, Pasadena, California, Laboratory of Dr. Name
Ph.D. Senior Research Fellow in Biology, 9/96-present
Auditory-motor interactions and interhemispheric coordination of pre-motor vocal activity in the zebra finch.
Ph.D. Research Fellow in Biology, 9/93-9/96
Auditory-motor interactions during song learning in the zebra finch.

University of Y, Laboratory of Dr. Name
Ph.D. Research Associate, 6/93-9/93
Temporal constraints in the regulation of neuronal survival by depolarization and neurotrophic factors.
Doctoral Student, 8/86-5/93
Regulation of Neuronal Survival through the Combined Action of Trophic Factors, Depolarization and Substratum.

Fox Chase Institute for Cancer Research, Philadelphia, Pennsylvania, Laboratory of Dr. Name
Ph.D. Research Technician, 5/85-8/85
Tissue specific expression of the major chicken Vitellogenin gene.

Centre Hospitalier Universitaire de Montigny-le-Tilleul, Belgium, Laboratory of Experimental Medicine and Immunology under Name, M.D./Ph.D.
Research Technician, 7/84-8/84
Effects of aging on the immune system.

PROFESSIONAL AFFILIATIONS

Society for Neurosciences. Member 1988-present
American Association for the Advancement of Science. Member 1987-present
American Society for Cell Biology. Student Member 1989-1993

HONORS AND AWARDS

Recipient of an NIDCD RO3 grant award, 1996-1998
National Research Service Award, National Institute of Health, 1993-1996
John H. Venable Research Scholarship, Colorado State University, 1990-1992
[Four additional awards follow.]

TEACHING EXPERIENCE

Neuroethology, **California Institute of Technology**, Spring 1997 (Guest Lectures)
Human Gross Anatomy, **University of X**, Spring 1989
Human Neuroanatomy, **University of X**, Fall 1987, Fall 1988

SEMINAR TALKS

Invited Speaker, Neuroscience Department, Baylor School of Medicine, Houston, Texas, January 1999
Invited Speaker, University of Nevada School of Medicine, Reno, Nevada, February 1995
Invited Speaker, Gordon Research Conference on Cell Contact and Adhesion, Proctor Academy, Andover, New Hampshire, July 1993
Invited speaker, Max-Planck-Institute for Psychiatry, Martinsried, Germany, April 1993
[Five additional talks follow.]

PUBLICATIONS

JOURNAL ARTICLES

Name, Candidate, Name and Name (1991) Sustained increase in intracellular calcium promotes neuronal survival J. Neurosci. 11: 2582-2587

Name, Candidate, Name, Name, Name and Name (1993) Role of intracellular calcium in NI-35-evoked collapse of neuronal growth cones. Science 259: 80-83

Candidate and Name (1993) Fibroblast growth factors, depolarization and substratum interact in a combinatorial way to promote neuronal survival. Dev. Biol. 158: 228-237
[Ten additional publications follow.]

REVIEW ARTICLES

Name and Candidate (1993) Filopodia as sensors for calcium signaling in neuronal growth cones. Neurosci. Facts 4: 23-24

Candidate (1998) Modulation by social context sheds new light on mechanisms of vocal production. Neuron 21: 645-647

Candidate and Name (1998a) Bilateral hemispheric coordination of birdsong. In Proceedings of the International Ornithology Congress, in press

ABSTRACTS

Name, Candidate, Name and Name (1990) Sustained increases in intracellular calcium promote neuronal survival in cultured chick ciliary ganglion neurons. J. Cell Biol Abst. 111: 244a

Candidate, Name, Name and Name (1991) CNS myelin neurite growth inhibitor NI-35 causes a large transient rise in intracellular calcium which precedes growth arrest and collapse of rat DRG growth cones. Soc. Neurosci. Abst 17: 927

[Twelve additional abstracts follow.]

Sample Science Vita
Used by ABD candidate for community college applications.

RUSSELL APPLICANT
Address
Phone
E-mail

EDUCATION

University of X   1996 to Present
- ABD, Biology, Completed coursework in 1998
  (Including Advanced Statistics, Urban Ecology Seminar)
- Available for full-time employment in January, 2000

Western Carolina University, Cullowhee, NC   1994-1996
- M.S. in Biology, Summa Cum Laude

James Madison University, Harrisonburg, VA   1986-1991
- B.S. in Biology
- Concentration: Entomology, Minors: English/Anthropology, Magna Cum Laude

TEACHING EXPERIENCE

University of X   Spring 2000
NSF Fellow
- Access Science Training Grant. Working with interdisciplinary team of science students and
  educators to plan and implement hands-on methods of teaching science and math to students in
  Philadelphia Public schools.

Community College of Philadelphia   1999-2000
Adjunct Faculty 1
- Introductory Biology. Survey of genetics, life systems, ecology and evolution for nonmajors.

University of X   1996-1999
Recitation Leader
- Vertebrate Physiology (3 sections). Lead class discussions on a variety of assigned papers
  stressing the relationship of form and function through comparisons of various animal systems.

Lab Instructor
- Head TA for General Biology B (2 semesters). Supervised and trained ten TAs, organized class
  schedules, advised students, prepared and graded exams.
- General Biology A (3 sections) and B (10 sections). Focused on concepts of evolutionary
  relationships and diversity of life through the study of development, morphology, and physiology.

University of X   July 1999
Lab Instructor
- Philadelphia Summer Science Academy (Microbiology Division). Instructed high school students in
  microbiology techniques. Students were selected from a national pool of applicants.

Western Carolina University   July 1996
Lecturer
- Human Physiology (1 Section). A course for pre-nursing and physical therapy students focused on
  the physiology of disease.

Russell Applicant, p. 2

Western Carolina University   1992-1994
Lab Instructor
- General Botany (1 section), General Zoology (2 sections), Introduction to Human Anatomy (2 sections), Introduction to Human Physiology (2 sections). Prepared and presented introductory lectures. Instructed students in exploring biological concepts through dissection and hands-on exercises.

Blue Ridge Community College   1991-1992
Lab Instructor
- General Biology I-II (2 sections each), Human Anatomy and Physiology I-II (1 section each). Assisted in instruction of classes comprising both direct high school graduates and students returning to school from the workplace.

James Madison University   1988-1981
Student Director
- Student Director of University Life Science Museum. Arranged natural-history displays, cared for live animals and arranged and conducted tours for visiting school children.

HONORS AND AWARDS

- Phi Kappa Phi, University of X Biology Graduate Student Association President (elected position) 1998-1999
- Award for Excellence in Teaching (Western Carolina University, 1996)
- Outstanding College Students of America
- Beta Beta Beta (Biology Honor Society)
- Sigma Tau Delta (International English Honor Society)
- Golden Key National Honor Society, Dean's List (James Madison University 1989-1991)

PUBLICATIONS

Candidate's Name, Name & Name, In Review: An Inventory of Grass Bald and Heath Bald Spider Assemblages and a Test of Species Richness Estimator Performances.

PERSONAL INTERESTS

Cooking, biking, hiking and camping, HTML, photography

Sample Engineering Vita
Candidate has substantial prior professional experience.

Ingrid Candidate

Office Address   Home Address
Office Phone   Home Phone
E-mail   Fax

Education

Doctor of Philosophy, Mechanical and Aerospace Engineering, 1999
X University, USA
Dissertation: "Aspects of the Failure of Patched Structures"
Advisor: Professor Name

Master of Science, Mechanical Engineering, 1990
Specialty: Mechanics of Materials, Solid Mechanics and Stress Engineering
The University of Linkoping, Linkoping, Sweden
"Surface Mounted Electronics in Extreme Environments: High Accelerations"
Advisor: Professor Name

Bachelor of Science, Mechanical Engineering, 1989
Specialty: Aerospace Engineering
The University of Linkoping, Linkoping, Sweden

Associate in Science, Mechanical Engineering, 1982
Orebro Institute of Technology, Orebro, Sweden

Research Interests

Mechanics of Solids and Structure (analytical and experimental)	Mechanics of Materials
Non-Linear Mechanics (including stability of structures)	Fracture and Delamination Mechanics
Smart Structures	Dynamics of Solids and Structures

Advanced and Traditional Materials (including composite materials, ceramics, and polymers)

Dissertation

Mechanical response, debonding characteristics, and instabilities of patched structures, such as aircraft repair and smart structures, are simulated via analytical modeling. The problems are approached from a uniform point of view, as propagating boundary problems in the calculus of variations, with the models for both flat and curved structures being formulated simultaneously. The formulation results in a self-consistent representation of the various intact and debonded segments of the composite structure comprised by the patch and the base structure. Issues such as stability of crack propagation and buckling of the composite structure are addressed. Critical geometric and materials performance parameters are identified and evaluated.

Teaching Experience

X University, USA
Lecturer   July 1995 - present
Fully responsible for course development and all aspects of instruction
• Mechanics of Materials, Summer 1999
• Engineering Mechanics: Dynamics, Spring 1999
[Three additional courses are listed.]
Teaching Assistant   Sept. 1994 - May 2000
• Engineering Mechanics: Dynamics, 5 sections, 1995 - 1998
• Engineering Mechanics: Statics, Fall 1995 (recitation)
• Aerospace Structures, Spring 1995
• Senior Laboratory, Fall 1994
Graduate Research Assistant   July 1996 - August 1997

Professional Experience

Program Manager, Advanced Materials Research, Rocky Hill, NJ   June 1994 - Sept. 1994
Developed and marketed a new version of AMR's software package GLS-PROP, a Microsoft Windows program that calculates the physical properties of glass from the chemical composition. Special sales and marketing efforts were initiated in Canada and Scandinavia.

Ingrid Candidate, p. 2

Technical Attaché Materials Science, Embassy of Sweden, Washington, DC   May 1992 - May 1994
Handled all embassy liaison activities concerning materials science and engineering between the United States and Sweden.
Working as a consultant, recruited sponsors and investigated a broad range of critical material topics. Conducted a national
study of ceramic material design methodologies for the production of high reliability monolithic and composite structure.

Research Engineer, Saab Missiles, Linkoping, Sweden   June 1990 - May 1992
Investigated and introduced Desk-Top Manufacturing (Rapid Prototyping) techniques to the design laboratory. Designed and
constructed circuit boards for use in high stress environments. Used FEA and fluid mechanics to model aerodynamic heating
of air-to-air missiles. Provided technical expertise and leadership for introduction of advanced materials into missile structures.
Specific expertise is in polymer composites, metal matrix composites, ceramics, and ceramic composites.
[Two other positions are listed.]

Committee Work
The Teaching Assistance Project, X University, Jan. 1996 - Dec. 1998

The Second Annual Teaching/Learning Conference, member of organizing committee, X University, Jan. 1998

"How Is It Really To Be a TA in Engineering?" Information for new Teaching Assistants, X University, August 1996, 1997

U.S. Work Permission
Swedish Citizen, U.S. Permanent Resident ("Green Card")

Publications
Refereed Journal Articles
"The Effect of Material Selection on the Debonding Behavior of Patched Structures," in preparation.

Candidate, Name, "Aspects of Thermally Induced Buckling of Patched Structures," Submitted (based on the paper AIAA-99-
1231, 40th AIAA/ASME/ASCE/AHS/ASC SDM Conference. St. Louis, MO, April 12 - 15, 1999, pp. 278-288).

"On the Behavior of a Class of Attached Plates During Cooling." Submitted to the International Journal of Non-Linear
Mechanics (32 manuscript pages, 32 figures).
 [Four more citations follow.]

Conference Presentations with Proceedings (refereed)
Candidate, Name, "Aspects of Thermally Induced Buckling of Patched Structures," AIAA-99-1231, 40th
AIAA/ASME/ASCE/AHS/ASC SDM Conference. St. Louis, MO, April 12 - 15, 1999, pp. 278-288.

Conference Presentations with Proceedings
[One citation follows.]

Book Chapters
Candidate, "Stress Analysis and Structural Design." Best Test Preparation for the PE: Mechanical Engineering Examination.
Research and Educational Association (REA), New Jersey. In press.

Selected Peer Reviewed Publications
Candidate, "Reliable Structural Materials from Advanced Ceramics." Report of the Swedish Technical Attachés, Washington
DC (1994).
[Five additional citations follow.]

Invited Presentations
"Swedish Research in Materials Science." U.S. Bureau of Mines, Washington DC, January 1994.
[Four additional presentations follow.]

Professional Societies
American Institute of Aeronautics and Astronautics (AIAA)   American Society of Mechanical Engineeers (ASME)
American Academy of Mechanics   Signa Xi

Sample Science Vita
Used for applications for postdoctoral fellowships.

DANIEL RESEARCHER

Home Address	Laboratory Address
Phone	URL
Fax	
E-mail	

EDUCATION

University of X, School of Medicine
Ph.D., Cell and Molecular Biology, expected, May 2001
Advisor: Advisor's Name

University of Illinois at Urbana-Champaign
B.S., Biochemistry, May 1993

PROFESSIONAL/RESEARCH EXPERIENCE

University of X, School of Medicine, Laboratory of Dr. Name
Graduate Student, Graduate Group in Cell and Molecular Biology, September, 1995-present

University of X, School of Medicine, Laboratory of Dr. Name
Lab Technician, June, 1994-August, 1995

University of Illinois at Chicago, Laboratory of Dr. Name
Lab Technician, September, 1993-June, 1994

University of Illinois at Urbana-Champaign, Laboratory of Dr. Name
Undergraduate Senior Thesis, August, 1992-May, 1993
Undergraduate Research Assistant, August, 1990-May, 1991, August, 1991-May, 1992

TEACHING EXPERIENCE

University of X
Teaching Assistant, January, 1997- May, 1997
Eukaryotic Gene Expression

HONORS AND AWARDS

University of X
Juan Grana Graduate Teaching Assistantship, January, 1997-May, 1997
National Research Service Award for Training in Cell and Molecular Biology, July, 1997-September, 1999

Daniel Researcher, p. 2.

PUBLICATIONS

Name, **Candidate**, and Name. 1994. Coexpression of exogenous and endogenous mouse mammary tumor virus RNA in vivo results in viral recombination and broadens the virus host range. J. Virol. 68: 5019-5026.

Name, Name, **Candidate**, and Name. 1995. Mouse mammary tumor viruses with functional superantigen genes are selected during in vivo infection. Proc. Natl. Acad. Sci. USA. 9295: 4828-4832.
[Three additional publications follow]

ABSTRACTS

Name, **Candidate**, and Name. Co-packaging of exogenous and endogenous mouse mammary tumor virus RNA in vivo broadens the virus host range and results in viral recombination. Retroviruses. Cold Spring Harbor Laboratory. Cold Spring Harbor, NY. May 1994.

Name, Name, Name, **Candidate**, Name, Name, and Name. Cloning of a putative cellular receptor for mmtv. Retroviruses. Cold Spring Harbor Laboratory. Cold Spring Harbor, NY. May 1996.
[Four additional abstracts follow.]

Sample Professional Vita, Education
Vita includes substantial professional experience.

LAURA APPLICANT
Home Address   Phone   E-mail Address

EDUCATION

Graduate School of Education
University of X
  Ph.D., Reading/Writing/Literacy   1998
  Dissertation: "Doing school and doing school differently: The perspectives of five adult
  learners on their past and current educational experiences"
  Dissertation committee: Dr. Name, Chairman; Dr. Name, Dr. Name

College of Arts and Sciences
University of Pennsylvania, Philadelphia, PA
  B.A., Elementary Education, cum laude   1985

UNIVERSITY TEACHING EXPERIENCE

State University of New Jersey, Rutgers, New Brunswick, NJ
  Assistant Professor of Adult Literacy Education   current
  Teach graduate students and conduct research on adult literacy education.

University of X   1998
  Lecturer, Adult Literacy
  Co-taught graduate-level course which encouraged students to consider the range of ways
  adult literacy is defined and conceptualized and how these have an impact on learners,
  practitioners, programs, funding and policy.

RESEARCH EXPERIENCE

Bureau of Adult Basic and Literacy Education, Pennsylvania Department of Education
Harrisburg, PA
  Project Director/Evaluation Director   1997-present
  Pennsylvania Professional Development System Evaluation
  Facilitated a year-long (1997-98) inquiry group of key stakeholders to develop an evaluation
  research design of the ABLE Bureau professional development delivery system in the state of
  Pennsylvania. Currently implementing evaluation, supervising team of seven research assistants.

University of Pennsylvania, Philadelphia, PA
  Research Assistant and Co-facilitator, Adult Literacy Practitioner Inquiry Project   1991-1995
  Co-facilitated, documented and reported on a two-year inquiry-based professional development
  activity designed for adult literacy practitioners. This project was developed to investigate
  practitioner inquiry as a promising form of staff development.

  Assistant Principal Investigator, Family Functioning and Literacy Competence in the
  Inner City: A Focus on the 1990 U.S. National Census   1991-1992
  Developed field protocol, collected data and managed all fieldwork related to qualitative study
  of citizen participation in completion of the U.S. Census. Collaboratively analyzed and
  reported on findings.

  Fieldworker, Family Functioning and Competence in the Inner City: A Focus on Adolescents   1990
  Conducted ethnographic field research with four families to compose community profile, identify
  neighborhood resources, document family utilization of resources and parental management
  styles in families of adolescents living in an "at risk" neighborhood.

  Research Assistant, Student Teachers as Researching Teachers (START)   1989-1991
  Participated in all aspects of documenting a reform-oriented teacher education program.
  Interviewed participants, coded data, aided in analysis and reporting.
  [One other role within this project is listed.]

Laura Applicant
Page 2

Research for Action, Philadelphia, PA
    Research Associate   1993-1996
    Designed and implemented evaluation designs, data collection and reporting for nonprofit
    organization specializing in evaluations of K-12 school reform efforts and professional
    development initiatives.
[Two other positions are listed.]

ADULT LITERACY PROFESSIONAL DEVELOPMENT FACILITATION

University of X, Philadelphia, PA
    Project Director, Pennsylvania Adult Literacy Practitioner Inquiry Network   1995-present
    Direct all aspects of state-wide initiative which adapts inquiry-based professional development
    approach developed and implemented locally in Philadelphia to a wide variety of local contexts
    throughout Pennsylvania.

    Co-facilitator/Research Assistant, Adult Literacy Practitioner Inquiry Project   1991-1995
    Co-facilitated, documented and reported on a two-year inquiry-based professional development
    activity designed for adult literacy practitioners. This project was developed to investigate
    practitioner inquiry as a promising form of professional development.

Mayor's Commission on Literacy, Philadelphia PA
    Facilitator, Adult Literacy Mentoring Inquiry Project   1993-1994
    Facilitated a year-long staff development project aimed at matching experienced adult literacy
    practitioner researchers with other practitioners interested in developing their practice using
    an inquiry-based approach.

    Co-facilitator, Program-based Adult Literacy Practitioner Inquiry Project   1992-1993
    Facilitated implementation of the Adult Literacy Practitioner Inquiry Project model for
    professional development at four area adult literacy programs.

ADULT LITERACY PRACTITIONER

Germantown Women's Educational Project, Philadelphia, PA
    Tutor   1994-1996
    Assisted teacher in all aspects of GED preparation class.

Center for Literacy, Philadelphia, PA
    Teacher   1988-1992
    Taught adult basic education classes with strong emphasis on literature-based reading and
    process-approach writing instruction arranged around thematic units.

    Program Developer   1988-1989
    Co-created 10-hour orientation workshop which introduced whole language and learner-
    centered literacy education strategies for adult learners and their volunteer tutors. Used as
    replacement for traditional training.

    Project Director   1988-1989
    Developed and implemented a project which trained, matched and supervised ten adult literacy
    learners who became peer tutors for other adults in the program.

    Tutor Trainer   1988-1989
    Facilitated nine-hour training workshops for volunteer literacy tutors.

    Coordinator   1987-1988
    Managed all aspects of a large one-to-one adult literacy tutoring program including assessment,
    instructional planning, student/tutor matching, and providing supervision and ongoing support.

[Three pages of **PUBLICATIONS** and **CONFERENCE PRESENTATIONS** follow.]

Sample Professional Vita, Business
Candidate has prior professional experience.

JOHN CANDIDATE, PH.D.
Home address
Home phone
Office phone
E-mail address

EDUCATION

Ph.D. in Human Resources and Industrial Relations; University of J, England, January, 1998
> *Dissertation Research on: Comparative International Human Resource Management and Industrial Relations Systems and Public Policy.*

Master's Degree in Public Administration; University of New Mexico, USA, December, 1994
> *Thesis Research on: and Course Concentration in Personnel Administration & Employment Law Awarded Postgraduate Certificate in Personnel Administration*

Bachelor's Degree in University Studies; University of New Mexico, USA, May, 1992

Associate in Arts Degree; University of Maryland, European Division, January, 1993

ACADEMIC HONORS

- Awarded Summer Research Fellowship, Rider University, 1999.
- Awarded Tuition Scholarship for Academic Merit by the Committee of Vice-Chancellors and Principals of the Universities of the United Kingdom for attendance to the University of X for Ph.D. studies, 1996.
- Received "The Ferrel Heady Best Professional Paper" Award from among MPA degree candidates, University of New Mexico, 1994.

[Includes two other awards.]

ACADEMIC POSTS AND TEACHING EXPERIENCE

Assistant Professor of Management and Human Resources, Rider University College of Business Administration, September 1998 to Present
Utilize a mix of traditional and distance learning/Internet-based learning methods. Courses taught include:

Introduction to Human Resources	Compensation Administration
Career Management	Internship in Human Resources
Human Resource Mgt. (MBA)	Legal Aspects of HR
Introduction to Labor Relations	

Visiting Assistant Professor, State University of New York, (SUNY) at Potsdam, Department of Economics, September 1997 to August 1998
Utilized a mix of traditional and distance learning/Internet-based learning methods. Courses taught include:

Employment Law	Collective Bargaining
Organizational Development	Contemporary Issues in Employment
Labor Law	Organizational Leadership
Internship in Labor Relations	Comparative/International Industrial Relations
Recruitment and Hiring Problems in Personnel Administration	

Lecturer, University of Maryland, European Division–England, October 1995 to January 1997
> *Courses taught include:* Human Resource Management, Problems & Analysis

Teaching Assistant, University of J, England, October 1995 to January 1997
> *Courses taught:* Research Methods and Data Analysis, Information Technology

J. Candidate, p. 2

Guest Lecturer (Teaching Assistant), University of New Mexico, School of Public Administration, Albuquerque NM, June 1992 to December 1994
Courses taught: Employment Law, Public Personnel Administration

Labor Educator, American Federation of State, County and Municipal Employees, AFL-CIO, Albuquerque, NM, December 1986 to April 1995
Education and Training Seminars Conducted:

Labor & Employment Law	Collective Bargaining
Grievance Handling & Representation	Alternative Dispute Resolution-Interest and Rights
	Arbitration and Mediation

UNIVERSITY SERVICE

Consult with the Office of the Associate Provost on the development of a comprehensive Occupational Health and Safety program for Rider University, 1999. Serve on the selection committee for recruitment of a Director of Environmental Health and Safety.
[Includes six other entries.]

PROFESSIONAL EXPERIENCE

Labor Management Relations Examiner, National Labor Relations Board, Indianapolis, IN, January 1997 to August 1997
Served in position while completing the Ph.D. dissertation. Mediated disputes between labor union officials and employers with regard to alleged unfair labor charges, and representation certification and decertification elections. Conducted fact-finding inquiries and investigations. [Lengthy description continues.]

Labor Relations Representative, American Federation of State, County and Municipal Employees Council 18, AFL-CIO, Albuquerque, NM, December 1986 to April 1995
Developed and negotiated as chief spokesperson, public and private sector contract proposals through the collective bargaining process. Directed, supervised and administered state-wide public and private sector labor relations organizing campaigns and representation programs. [Lengthy description continues.]

REFEREED ACADEMIC JOURNAL PUBLICATIONS

Journal of Labor Research (Forthcoming). *Public Sector Union Democracy: A Comparative Analysis.* With Name.

Labor Law Journal (Forthcoming, Winter 1999). *Union Salting and Worker Loyalty Since Town & Country: A Legal Analysis of New Industry Strategies.* With Name.
[Seven citations follow.]

BOOK CHAPTERS

Annual Editions: Management 99/00, 7th Edition (February 1999). Chapter 6. *Covert Union Organizing: Beware the Trojan Horse.* McGraw Hill. Adopted from the article of the same title previously published in **Workforce,** May 1998. Name, ed.

RESEARCH & PUBLICATIONS IN PROGRESS

American Labor Union Organizing and the Law (with Name). Presentation invited by the Hungarian Academy of Sciences and Eötvös Lóránd University. March 2000.
[Five citations follow.]

J. Candidate, p. 3

PUBLICATIONS IN PROFESSIONAL JOURNALS

HR World (January/February 2000). Invited column, *Outsourcing in CEE.* 3(1), London.
[Fifteen citations follow.]

PAPERS PRESENTED AT CONFERENCES

Society of Human Resource Management SHRM (April 1998). Invited paper presented at the Institute for International Human Resource Management Conference. *Labor Relations, Employment and Labor Movements in the New Central and Eastern Europe.* Dallas, Texas.
[Two citations follow.]

CONFERENCE PUBLICATIONS

Arbitrálás–Amerikai Módra (Arbitration–The American Model). By Candidate and Name, 1994. Edited, translated and published by the Ministry of Labor, Institute of Labor Research, Budapest, Hungary.

RESEARCH INTERESTS

- Employment and labor law
- Labor and industrial relations in the private and public sectors
- Workplace behavior and conflict, and conflict resolution
- The transition of human resource management and industrial relations systems in the transitional economies in central and eastern Europe.

RELATED ACADEMIC & RESEARCH ACTIVITIES

- Served as conference proceedings reviewer for the Western Academy of Management, 1999.
- Served as conference proceedings reviewer for the International Association of Management, 1999.
- Served as article reviewer for the journal *Management Development Forum*, 1999.
- Invited by the International Labor Organization (Central and East European Division) to participate in a symposium on "Negotiated Wage Policies," with the intent of developing alternative policy solutions to the diminishing real wage problem and promoting collective bargaining in the transitional economies. Budapest, Hungary, November 1995.
- Admitted to the National Panel of Employment Law Arbitrators, American Arbitration Association, 1993.

PROFESSIONAL DEVELOPMENT AND TRAINING

Writing Across the Curriculum – A seminar to improve the development of writing assignments in the classroom, Rider University, January 1999 - April 1999.
[Seven entries follow.]

MEMBERSHIP AND AFFILIATIONS
[Five memberships listed with dates.]

REFERENCES

[Contact information for five recommenders follows.]

Sample Professional Vita, Communications
Web-based. Linked items are underlined.

Darren Candidate

URL
[Top of page has links to each section of the vita, as well as a link to <u>HOME</u>, the candidate's personal Web site, which included an e-mail address. Some people choose not to include other contact information on Web-based vitas.]

Education

<u>UNIVERSITY OF X</u>
<u>The Y School for Communication</u>
Ph.D. Candidate, September 1995–Present
Cumulative G.P.A.: 4.0

M.A., August 1995
Thesis: *Rising Frustrations Revisited: The Effects of Market Messages on Disadvantaged Youths*
Cumulative G.P.A.: 3.8

<u>UNIVERSITY OF VIRGINIA</u>, Charlottesville, Virginia
B.A. with Highest Distinction, May 1993
Double Major: Rhetoric and Communication/Foreign Affairs
Minor: African-American and African Studies
G.P.A. in First Major: 3.8. Cumulative G.P.A.: 3.4

Research Experience

Research Associate
<u>The Y School for Communication</u>, University of X
Operationally defined and assessed the <u>quality of children's television</u>. Developed and conducted a content analysis of children's television programming. Reviewed relevant research literature.
Spring 1996 - Summer 1996

Research Intern
Marketing and Media Research Department
<u>Children's Television Workshop</u>, New York, New York
Completed a secondary analysis of market research data, tracked competitor performance, assisted with the testing and development of new products.
Summer 1995
[Two additional experiences follow.]

Teaching Experience

Children and Television, Lecturer
Undergraduate Course, University of X, Summer 1996
After a general overview of the child development and mass media effects literature, taught on the cognitive, behavioral, socio-cultural, and business effects of television on children.

Navigating the Internet, Lecturer
<u>Summer Academy Course</u>, University of X, Summer 1996
Taught how an amalgam of governmental, academic, and business institutions coalesced to create the Internet. Discussed its current technical configuration, the cultural impact of the new technology, and various policy issues surrounding its governance. Taught students how to use electronic mail, newsgroups, file transfer protocol, and create Web pages.
[Three additional teaching experiences follow.]

Darren Candidate, p. 2

Additional Experience

Mayoral Intern, Mayor Edward G. Rendell, <u>Philadelphia, Pennsylvania</u>
Summer 1994
Worked in the Office for Special Needs Housing on several projects to assist the homeless of Philadelphia. Designed and implemented the city's outreach program for the homeless during extreme summer weather conditions, assisted with various grant proposals, including the Innovative Housing Project for which the city was awarded $500 million, and compiled public relations materials for the office.
[Four additional experiences follow.]

Papers

<u>Interactive Media–Communication Technologies for the 21st Century</u>. Media Development 41.4 (1994): 18-22.

<u>Mídia interativa: televisão no século 21</u>. Comunicação & Sociedade Ano XII– n. 21 Junho 1994.

<u>Television and Cognitive Development</u>. Presented at the annual convention of the Speech Communication Association, November 1996, San Diego, California.

<u>Distorted Looking Glass: Mass Media Dysfunctions in Consumer Socialization</u>. Presented at the annual convention of the Speech Communication Association, November 1996, San Diego, California
[Two additional papers follow.]

Skills

Qualitative: Focus Groups, Content Analysis, In-Depth Interview
Quantitative: ANOVA, MANOVA, Factor Analysis, Reliability Analysis, Structural Equation Modeling, Time Series Analysis, Mean Comparisons, Expectancy Table Analysis, Path Analysis, Logistic Regression, Regression, Audience Analysis
[Additional lists for Statistics, Spreadsheet, Word Processing, Database, Internet, and Presentation follow.]

Honors

Competitive Paper Award, Speech Communication Association, Mass Communication Division, <u>Distorted Looking Glass: Mass Media Dysfunctions in Consumer Socialization</u> (November 1996).

Top Student Paper Award, International Communication Association, Information Systems Division. From a field of over 50 competitive papers, <u>Argumentative Skill: A Measure of Schema Development</u> was recognized as the best paper written by a student. (May 1995).
[Eight additional awards follow.]

Leadership

Graduate Student Council, The Y School for Communication, Fall 1996
Served as a liaison between the student body and the administration, developed writing workshop program, initiated community service projects, secured capital goods for student body, and organized social events.

Jewish and African-American Relations, University of Virginia, Fall 1990–Spring 1993
Co-founded and co-chaired an organization to bring together individuals from the Jewish and African-American communities. Organized educational, cultural, and social events. Gave talks on the need for better relations.

[Community Service section follows.]

Sample Fine Arts Vita

ALBERTO ARTIST

Address
Phone
E-Mail

EDUCATION

Master of Fine Arts, Painting, Z College, University of Y, New York, NY, 1992 (studied with Artist's Name, Artist's Name, Artist's Name, Artist's Name, and Artist's Name)

Bachelor of Fine Arts, Painting, Portland School of Art (now Maine College of Art), 1982, Portland, ME (studied with Artist's Name, Artist's Name, Artist's Name, and Artist's Name)

SELECTED SOLO EXHIBITIONS

- The Casements, Ormond Beach, FL, 1999
- Art Vivant Gallery, Charlotte, NC, 1997
- Jay County Arts Council, Portland, IN, 1997
- Richart Gallery, New York, NY, 1997
- Empire State Building, New York, NY, 1997
- John Jay College Gallery, New York, NY, curated by Name, 1995

[Five additional exhibitions follow.]

SELECTED GROUP EXHIBITIONS

- "Clinton AKA Hell's Kitchen" Gallery@49, New York, NY
- "Abstraction Index," Condeso-Lawler Gallery, New York, NY (with Name, Name, Name, Name, and others)
- Faculty Show, Westchester Art Workshop, White Plains, NY (with Name, Name, and others)

[Sixteen additional exhibitions follow.]

SELECTION OF PUBLIC COLLECTIONS

- The Metropolitan Museum of Art
- Reader's Digest Corporation
- Alberta College of Art and Design

[Three additional collections follow.]

TEACHING EXPERIENCE

Adjunct Assistant Professor, Hunter College, (CUNY), New York, NY, Jan. 1994-present
- Color as Communication
- Painting 200

[Two additional courses are listed.]

Adjunct Professor, State University of New York (SUNY), Westchester, Art Workshop, White Plains, NY, Jan. 1993-present
- Introductory Painting
- Intermediate Painting

[Six additional courses are listed.]

University of Vermont, Burlington, VT, 1984-85
- Introductory Painting
- Advanced Painting

Alberto Artist, p. 2

Portland School of Art, Teaching Assistant, Portland, ME, 1982
- Figure Drawing

St. Joseph of the Holy School, New York, NY, Sept. 1998 - present
- Developed art program and taught art part-time to grades 1-8, grant position

PAPERS PRESENTED

Conference Speaker, College Art Association, Toronto, paper title: "A Dystopia of Color Education in a Utopia of Color Experience" (seminar included Name and Name), 1998.
Conference Speaker at Association Internationale de la Couleur (AIC), Goteborg, Sweden, paper title: "Constructs of Color Evidence: The Psychological Ordering of Color Relationships in the Teaching of Color Theory," 1996.
[Four additional papers follow.]

VISITING ARTIST RESIDENCIES

- Alberta College of Art and Design, Calgary, Alberta, invited by Name, Name, and Name
- Glen Oaks Community College, Centreville, MI, invited by Name

PUBLICATIONS

- Due out June 2000, *Color Mixing: The 12-Hue Method*, Rockport Publishers
- More than 30 published articles for magazines, journals, and book chapters
- Monthly column in *American Artist* magazine on Methods & Materials

COMMUNITY INVOLVEMENT

- National Public Radio, interview on aspects of color, "Weekday," KUOW, Seattle, WA
- Curator for painting exhibition "In a New Light," Peekskill, NY
- Consultant for All Japan Fashion Institute, NY, Japan
- Panelist, Queens Council on the Arts

AWARDS

- E.D. Foundation Grant, 1996
- Manhattan Graphics Center Grant, New York, NY, 1995
[Eight additional awards follow.]

MEMBERSHIP

- College Art Association
[Three additional memberships follow].

ADMINISTRATIVE AND RELATED EXPERIENCE

- Christie's Auction House, New York, NY, Librarian Assistant (oversaw interns), 1992-94
- New York Philharmonic Symphony Society, New York, NY, Assistant Archivist, 1990-92
- Dance Theatre of Harlem, Librarian/Archivist, 1989-90
- New York Shakespeare Festival, Associate Archivist, 1987-89
- Carnegie Hall, Publicity Coordinator, 1985-87
- Numerous full and part time jobs to pay the rent, 1976-85

Sample Business Resume of a Science Ph.D.

Vijay Applicant

Address   Phone/Fax
URL   E-mail address

Objective: A position in business consulting.

SKILLS

Business
- Evaluated, selected, and marketed new technologies for the Center for Technology Transfer at the University of X. Researched and analyzed the market for each technology. Selected potential licensee companies to target marketing efforts. Wrote concise, non-technical reports on each technology for marketing purposes.
- Controlled and administered the $265,000 budget of the Graduate and Professional Student Assembly (GAPSA). Created the annual budget for GAPSA and updated the budget categories to better reflect the mission of the organization.

Leadership and Teamwork
- First Vice-Chair of GAPSA, the student government for the 10,000 graduate students at the University of X. As a member of the GAPSA executive board, a team of nine committed individuals, participation in GAPSA events was increased by 400% and press coverage by 300%. Served as chair of a standing committee.
- Advised the President and Provost of the University of X as a graduate representative to the University Council, the highest governmental body at the university.
- Collaborated with chemists, material scientists, and physicists at the University of X and in Germany and France.

Computer
- Platforms: Unix (SunOS, Linux, AIX), DOS, Windows, Windows 95
- Applications: Word processing (MS-Word, WordPerfect), spreadsheets and financial (MS-Excel, QuattroPro, Lotus 1-2-3, Quicken), text formatting (Latex/Tex)
- Programming: C, BASIC and Asyst (scientific language), graphing and image processing (PV-Wave/IDL, SigmaPlot) and World Wide Web (html)

EMPLOYMENT HISTORY

Center for Technology Transfer, *University of X,* Associate	2000 - present
Laboratory for Research on the Structure of Matter, *University of X,* Graduate Research Assistant	1997 - present
Physics Department, *University of X,* Graduate Teaching Assistant	1996 – 1998
Physics Department, *Queen's University,* Undergraduate Research Assistant	1994 - 1996
Dominion Soils Engineering, *Concrete and Soils Laboratory,* Geotechnician	1992 – 1994

ACADEMIC ACHIEVEMENTS AND AWARDS

- Measured and analyzed x-ray diffraction from various liquid crystals and polymer thin films.
- Presented research results to peer physicists and chemists at academic conferences.
- Published several academic papers in peer reviewed journals of physics and chemistry.
- Awarded the Chairman's Teaching Award for outstanding teaching of undergraduate physics laboratory courses.
- Distinguished as a Canada Scholar and as a Tricolor Scholar.

EDUCATION

Ph.D. Candidate, Physics, *University of X*	expected December 2001
B.Sc. Honors, Physics, *Queen's University,* Kingston, Ontario, Canada	May 1996

United States permanent resident, citizen of Canada and the European Union.

Sample Business Resume of a Humanities Ph.D.

BRENDAN APPLICANT, Ph.D.

Address
Telephone Number (Home)
Fax Number
E-mail Address

Career Objective

- Consultant in corporate development and business transformation.

Summary of Qualifications

- Extensive experience in research, information management, and communication.
- Proven effectiveness in presentation and communication.
- Initiatives in program innovation and institutional transformation.
- Strong track record in individual and group motivation.
- Recent training in business skills and concepts.
- Sustained record of individual achievement.

Work Experience

- Assistant Professor, Bard College, New York. Program innovator and director. Teacher, advisor, mentor. Organize presentations by visiting lecturers, manage lecturer budget, oversee publicity. Committee and program member. Awarded research grant. Give public lectures, attend professional conferences, publish essays and reviews. July 1995–present.
- Co-director of private investment group. Responsible for allocating and managing $500,000 in assets. August 1998–present.
- Assistant Professor, Université de Montréal, Canada. Teacher, advisor, graduate studies committee member. Received competitive research grant. July 1993–June 1995.

Education

- SUNY New Paltz, New York. Course work in marketing, accounting, management, and economics. Department of Business Administration. GPA 4.0. 1998.
- University of X. Ph.D. in English and American Literature. 1993.
- Brown University, Rhode Island. B.A., English Literature, with Honors. Summa cum laude. Undergraduate prizes. GPA 3.87. 1986.

Skills

- Focus on defining problems and researching solutions.
- Full engagement with projects from inception to completion.
- Effective synthesis of details and broader vision.
- Independent thinking.
- Management of personnel and corporate structure.
- Evaluation of individual and group dynamics and performance.
- French proficiency.
- Word processing, database, spreadsheet, and Internet.

References available upon request.

Sample Professional Resume of a Social Science Ph.D.

ESTELLE CANDIDATE
Address, Phone Number, E-Mail Address

OBJECTIVE
Position with organization working with underserved and/or third world populations carrying out qualitative and quantitative analysis for culturally appropriate program implementation and evaluation.

SKILLS
Extensive experience in qualitative ethnographic research; skilled in quantitative and epidemiological analysis. Experience in curriculum development, research design and community-based strategic planning. Effective public speaker with ability to write clearly and concisely under deadlines.

EDUCATION

UNIVERSITY OF X, Ph.D., Folklore and Ethnography, 2000
> *Areas of research*: Cultural and medical anthropology, indigenous religious medical traditions, applied ethnography, professional and caring ethics, definitions of community
> *Dissertation*: An Ethics of Care: Politics and Religion in American Indian Health

UNIVERSITY OF OKLAHOMA, M.P.H., Epidemiology, 1999

HARVARD UNIVERSITY, A.B., History and Literature, *magna cum laude*, 1991
Certificate, Latin American Studies, 1991
> *Honors Thesis:* Traces of Disappearance: Contemporary Chilean Poetry and the Experience of Dictatorship
UNIVERSIDAD CATOLICA DE CHILE, Literature and History, 1989

EXPERIENCE IN COMMUNITY HEALTH

USPHS INDIAN HEALTH SERVICE, Oklahoma City Area Office, 1999-March 2000; June-September 1998
Epidemiologist/Consultant
- Analyzed five years of diabetes mellitus clinical audit statistics for all Indian health facilities in Oklahoma area.
- Wrote reports summarizing statistical and clinical information on American Indian diabetics included in the audit.
- Presented findings to key IHS administrators, physicians and public health personnel.

NATIVE AMERICAN PREVENTION RESEARCH CENTER, University of Oklahoma Health Sciences Center
ASSOCIATION OF AMERICAN INDIAN PHYSICIANS, Oklahoma City, 1999-2000
Consultant/Public Health Education
- Researched and collected culturally appropriate diabetes education materials for American Indians in Oklahoma area for national health education initiative.
- Wrote report on findings and determined potential for use of materials in national/local television and radio spots.

HEALTH AGENCY TRAINING, Epidemiology and Biostatistics Department, University of Oklahoma Health Sciences Center, 1997-1998
Public Health Training Specialist
- Developed curriculum materials for basic epidemiology courses in seven state region for health department personnel.
- Developed materials and coordinated train-the-trainer courses and area steering committee meetings.
- Created web site of training schedule and Internet links to state health agencies and national health databases.

CHEYENNE AND ARAPAHO TRIBES and USPHS INDIAN HEALTH SERVICE, 1996-1997
Strategic Plan Coordinator
- Documented one year of bimonthly meetings between Indian Health Service professionals, tribal health board, tribal business committee and health workers concerning problems with the Indian health services and their potential solutions.
[Two additional responsibilities are listed.]

Estelle Candidate, p. 2

PENN STATE COLLEGE OF MEDICINE, DEPARTMENT OF HUMANITIES, 1995-1997
Qualitative Research Analyst
- Created case studies from qualitative field research for four-year diversity training curriculum.
- Researched American Indian and Mexican American health beliefs.
- Conducted fieldwork in tribal communities in southwestern Oklahoma and facilitated tribal/community advocacy.
[One additional experience follows.]

TEACHING EXPERIENCE

REDLANDS COMMUNITY COLLEGE, El Reno, OK
Instructor/Lecturer
   Introduction to Humanities, Introduction to Sociology, English Composition I & II. Fall 1996-Summer 1997

UNIVERSITY OF X
Teaching Associate
   Writing About Fiction, *Cross-cultural experiences in illness, healing and death*, Fall 1994; *Magical realism and beyond* (Latin American authors in translation), Spring 1995
   - Created syllabi, developed written assignments, taught college writing skills.
[One additional listing is included.]

RELATED EXPERIENCE

NEW JERSEY HISTORICAL SOCIETY and AFRO AMERICAN HISTORICAL AND GENEALOGICAL
SOCIETY, INC., NJ
Grant Writer—Ethnicity and Medicine, March-June 1995
- Authored segment of successful grant to restore house and set groundwork for creating museum.
- Researched and wrote about Dr. James Still (1812-1885), "Black Doctor of the Pines," giving historical background on professionalization of medicine, race relations, alternative therapies.

APPRENTICE TO LAY MIDWIFE, Name, June 1992-May 1993
   - Assisted at home births, prenatal exams, and birthing classes.
[One additional listing is included.]

FELLOWSHIPS AND AWARDS

The Outstanding Student Award, College of Public Health, University Of Oklahoma Health Sciences Center, 1999
Alpha Epsilon Lambda. "For excellence in service to graduate and professional school students through outstanding scholarship, character, and leadership." Elected member, 1999
[Seven additional listings are included.]

LANGUAGES AND COMPUTER ABILITY

Fluent: Spanish. Reading ability: Portuguese, French, Italian
EPI-INFO, SAS, EXCEL, PowerPoint, Microsoft Word, WordPerfect, PageMaker

INTERNATIONAL EXPERIENCE

Chile 1/89-10/90: Attended one year of university study, worked as translator for the Relatives of the Detained and Disappeared, organized itinerary, and translated for investigative reporting in northern Chile.
Bolivia and Argentina 4/90-6/90; Spain, Poland, Czech Republic, Greece 9/88-12/88: Low budget travel
Mexico 3/93: Book buyer for Spanish language bookstore; 6/85-8/85: American Field Service exchange student

[PUBLICATIONS AND PRESENTATIONS follow on a separate page.]

Chapter 11
Additional Application Materials

About Your Research

Dissertation Abstract

You may be asked to provide an abstract of your dissertation as part of the initial screening process for a faculty position. Or you may wish to provide it with your application whether or not you are specifically asked for it.

Your abstract should conform to the conventions for your field. It is usually one or two pages long. Make the abstract, and therefore your dissertation, sound interesting and important. Use the active rather than the passive construction whenever possible, and stress findings and conclusions where they exist. Rather than saying, "A possible relationship between x and y was studied," say, for example, "Demographic data indicate that x increased as y declined."

Briefly indicate how your research fits into a broader context to answer the implicit "Why should anyone care?" question that may be asked of any piece of research. Someone who reads your abstract should have a clear idea of what your work entailed and want to ask you more about it. Write, rewrite, and seek critiques from your advisor and others in your department until you're satisfied that the abstract will achieve this effect.

Statement of Research Plans

Like an abstract, this short summary (usually one or two pages) may be requested as part of the application process. At other times, you may choose to include it to strengthen your application. Preparing this document is wonderful practice for interviews (see Chapter 14, "Interviewing"), because employers are keenly interested in what you plan to do in the future. It is not expected that you will have begun to do research beyond your dissertation, only that you will have begun to think about it coherently.

If you plan to publish your dissertation as several articles or turn it into a book, you may mention that fact briefly. Be sure, however, to discuss plans for research that extend beyond your dissertation. If your plans sound simply like extensions of your dissertation, or if you use phrases like "We do this," then you risk giving the impression that you view your plans as an extension of your advisor's research and that you have not begun to think of yourself as an independent researcher.

Give a brief context for your research interests, including how they fit into work others have done, and then discuss your plan for investigation. It is very important to communicate a sense that your research will follow logically from what you have done and be different, important, and innovative. Describing plans at an appropriate level of generality/specificity may require some rewriting and feedback from faculty members. A research plan so specific that one article could complete it is too limited, but one that includes a whole area of study, for example, "labor economics," is too general. If you will require substantial facilities and/or external funding for your research, include that in your discussion. If you've identified funding organizations likely to support your research plans, indicating that this is the case will make your plan sound more credible.

If this document makes the reader want to ask you further questions, even challenge you, it has done its job admirably, because it has helped make it seem that an interview with you would be lively and interesting. Write as clearly and concisely as you can.

While of course it would be unethical for members of a hiring committee to appropriate a candidate's detailed research plans for their own research, candidates have at least suspected this has happened to them. Find your own balance between talking about your research plans specifically enough to be credible and abstractly enough to protect your interest in your own creative ideas.

Dissertation Chapter or Other Writing Sample

These documents are usually requested only after an initial screening and it isn't to your advantage to send them unsolicited. In deciding what to send, choose something that is interesting and stands on its own, even if it is part of a longer document. If you send a long chapter, you might want to enclose a note directing readers' attention to a particular section of it, since, in reality, many committee members will skim documents. Check with your advisor and other faculty members to see what work would represent you best. Apart from a dissertation chapter, it is usually better to send published, rather than unpublished, material.

About Your Teaching

Statement of Teaching Philosophy

While the word "philosophy" is often used as part of the name for this document, it is perhaps better thought of as a brief essay that will give a hiring committee an idea of what you actually do in the classroom. You will need to make some general statements, but make sure to include examples that illustrate what you mean by them. If at all possible, describe things you have already done, or at least seen in practice, rather than give examples which are entirely hypothetical. If students responded well to an approach, say so. Avoid cliches, buzzwords, and "hot button" words that may immediately cause the hiring committee to identify you as something you are not. However, do not hesitate to express your ideas simply and directly.

For ideas, try to look at statements written by others in your department as well as those written by applicants to your department, if those are available to you. Look at the Web pages of hiring institutions and read their statements of philosophy, missions, and goals to help you get a sense of some of the dimensions which are frequently addressed when people talk about teaching.

Teaching Portfolio

Sometimes, particularly after making a "first cut," candidates are asked for additional materials about teaching, such as a syllabus for a course you have taught or a proposal for a course you would like to teach. Some candidates compile "teaching portfolios," which can include syllabi and other materials developed for courses, comments from students, and self-evaluations of one's teaching. While these can be nice enhancements, they are rarely required and should not be submitted unsolicited at the first stage of application.

However, Web-based versions (discussed in more detail in Chapter 12) should always be mentioned on your vita or in your cover letter. Compared to paper copy, they are much less burdensome for hiring committees.

Evidence of Successful Teaching

Some job ads ask for "evidence of successful teaching." While such a requirement is obviously open-ended, it's a good idea to include something that involves external evaluation of your teaching. You might, for instance, present a faculty member with all your teaching evaluations, if your institution uses them, and ask that person to summarize them into a shorter letter. The author of the letter can interpret whatever numerical system is generally used by your institution. For example, if instructors of a required chemistry course on average receive scores of only 3 on a scale of 5, the person writing the letter can explain that your score of 3.7 is truly impressive. If you've received teaching awards, you or someone writing about your teaching can put those into context as well.

Videotape of Your Teaching

As institutions try to control their hiring costs, they increasingly want to know more and more about candidates before paying to bring them to campus. On a growing number of occasions, institutions that care very much about the quality of teaching are asking candidates not only to write about their teaching philosophy but also to send a videotape of their classroom teaching. Generally, the tape will be requested after the initial pool of applicants has been narrowed down to a smaller number. While there is no guarantee that you will be asked for a tape, if you are concentrating your search on institutions oriented to teaching you should probably go ahead and prepare one so that you can have it immediately ready if it's requested.

You are more likely to be asked for a short tape than for a tape of a full-length class. If you want to emphasize the breadth of your teaching abilities, you might choose to compile a tape from shorter classroom segments. If you don't care to prepare a tape in advance of your applications, be prepared to produce one on short notice, if necessary. If you are currently teaching a course, you could easily produce a tape quickly simply by arranging for part of one of your regular class sessions to be taped. If you are not currently teaching, you might want to find someone who would let you use part of his or her class time for this purpose.

Other Things That Might Be Required

If you are in a visual field, such as fine arts or architecture, a portfolio or slides of your work will always be required, as may be an "artist's statement." Their preparation is beyond the scope of this discussion, but take them very seriously. Check with your professional association. For example, the College Art Association <www.collegeart.org> gives excellent advice on slide preparation. Your advisor will also be able to provide you with guidelines. Seek out his or her critiques, and ask others for theirs as well.

A Note About the Sample Materials That Follow

The following examples, generously volunteered by real candidates, are provided to give you an idea of what such materials look like. We have not changed them in any respect except to omit the authors' names and correct a few typographical errors. Custom in your own field might well dictate that yours should be quite different in style, language, or appearance.

Sample Dissertation Abstract, Humanities

Emigration and its Effects in Meiji-era Yamaguchi Prefecture

Dissertation Abstract
by Aaron Candidate
Advisor: Professor Name
Completion Expected: August 1999

Between 1885 and 1940 almost a million Japanese emigrated overseas, approximately half of them permanently. Over half of the emigrants came from five prefectures, including Yamaguchi; fully one in ten emigrants from Meiji Japan (1868-1912) were from Yamaguchi. Even within these high-emigration prefectures, regional variation was intense: well over 90% of emigrants from Yamaguchi prefecture came from three counties in southeastern Yamaguchi. Earnings of overseas laborers reached millions of dollars and yen, making labor Yamaguchi's most important international export. My hypothesis is that international emigration represents an alternative to the urban and industrial development of central Japan; Yamaguchi, as a result, will exhibit a socio-economic pattern similar to prefectures near to, but not part of, the Tokyo-Osaka development corridor.

The economy of Yamaguchi in the early Meiji period was slow to change from traditional agriculture and fishing to manufacturing and more profitable specialty crops. Southeastern Yamaguchi was the poorest area, by most measures. It did not, however, exhibit the economic stratification and widespread poverty that came to many other rural areas of Meiji Japan. Rather, the late Meiji saw a boom of independent farming and fishing families, and substantial growth of small businesses fueled by emigration income. By the 1920s, Yamaguchi was importing laborers from elsewhere in Japan to work in its agricultural and industrial enterprises. The capital for this change came largely from the government and from individual savings. The role of the traditionally prominent wealthy landlord class is more muted in Yamaguchi than elsewhere.

Social change came slowly to Yamaguchi. There was little difference between the demographic profiles of Yamaguchi prefecture and Japan's other rural areas when emigration began in 1885. Emigrants were reasonably well distributed within families, and although initial emigrants were heavily male, those who remained overseas were joined by increasing numbers of unmarried (or picture bride) female emigrants in the early 1900s. The cosmopolitanism of the high emigration regions does not seem to have resulted in changes in social structure or village leadership: the leveling effect of emigrant incomes may have diluted the authority of traditional leaders, but their role in facilitating emigration counteracted that effect. Though there are sporadic accounts of emigrant community and individual donations to schools, there is little evidence of sustained differences between high emigration regions and the rest of Yamaguchi in educational development. Contact with Christianity in Hawaii and California does not seem to have resulted in higher numbers of Christians in Yamaguchi: rather, there were substantial donations to local Shinto and Buddhist institutions. Emigration was an economic phenomenon much more than it was a social or cultural phenomenon.

There is a small amount of research in both Japanese and English on the government and corporate mechanisms of emigration in Japan, Hawaii and the Americas. Local histories of high emigration regions in Japan, however, sometimes entirely fail to mention the international connections and influences on the community, and never integrate emigration into the social or economic development of the region. This dissertation contributes to the slowly growing body of English-language scholarship on Japanese local and social history, by looking at a region rarely studied beyond 1868. It also places emigration in the context of a detailed history of local social and economic development in order to clarify issues of regionality and change in Meiji Japan.

Sample Research Statement, Social Science/Professional

ESTELLE CANDIDATE
Address
Phone Number E-Mail Address

STATEMENT OF RESEARCH INTERESTS

Current Research

Public Health

Currently I am working with the Native American Prevention Research Center and the Association of American Indian physicians to gather and assess culturally appropriate diabetes education materials for American Indians. This involves research and professional networking in Oklahoma, Kansas, Arkansas, and Missouri. The education materials that I am compiling will contribute to a national database of diabetes education materials and will provide a description of current health education services and suggest areas for education enhancement.

I also work on contract with the Indian Health Service to analyze five years of diabetes audit data for the Oklahoma City Area Office. This consists of epidemiological analysis and writing extensive reports to be distributed to the various service units and individual facilities.

Ethnography of Medicine

My dissertation *The Ethics of Care: Politics and Religion in American Indian Health* draws on several years of field research among southern plains American Indians, physicians, community health representatives, public health nurses, and Indian Health Service professionals in western Oklahoma. My analysis utilizes theories of behavioral science including applied medical ethnography, sociology, and anthropology of medicine. I argue that Southern Cheyenne ethics of care, based on notions of reciprocity and generosity, are almost diametrically opposed to the values of commodified health care they experience within the Indian Health Service and in medical care in general. Moreover, the distanced professionalism in ethnography and health research preclude participation in this caring ethic demanded of researchers in the field. In both professional realms, physicians and health researchers have much to gain by adapting their skills and professionalism to embrace potential social involvement with patients and communities.

I plan to transform my dissertation into a book on American Indian health politics in Oklahoma.

Future Research Goals

I plan to carry out NIH/CDC funded research and community intervention programs concerning American Indian chronic health issues such as heart disease, diabetes, and cancer. With my extensive research experience in American Indian health beliefs and behaviors, my research will include these social variables (along with the standard socioeconomic and etiologic variables) in the design of my research methods, and they will guide my promotion and prevention strategies. Through my ethnographic and public health field research I have already established a large network of professional relationships that will aid my plans for research and community intervention.

I am especially committed to including American Indians (both lay and professional) in every stage of the research and community interventions—from the conceptualization and planning stages, to the implementation, to the field research and questionnaires, to writing up results. I feel strongly that the results should be presented to the communities in ways that they understand and can utilize in the future. Moreover, many American Indian communities have great interest in acting on health research results to create community programs of their own. I hope to foster such reciprocal relationships between colleagues at the College of Public Health and American Indian communities to help provide professional expertise to help communities carry out their own research and to create programs of their own design.

Sample Research Statement, Social Science

Statement of Research Interests
B. G. Researcher

I have two primary research interests: impacts of international migration on children growing up in Mexico, and income inequality in the United States.

- I continue my research on how the prevalence of household and community-level international and internal migration affects children's education, employment, and migration. Prospective research includes examining the impact of migration on social change in Mexico, and exploring causes of education outcomes of "second generation" U.S. immigrants.

- I have begun new research evaluating income inequality in the U.S. over time using relative distribution methods. Professor Name and I are currently examining the gender gap in earnings as well as differences between immigrants' and natives' earnings.

My dissertation explored two important and under-researched topics on globalization: how temporary migration flows to developed countries alter the human capital investment calculus for children in developing countries, and how assimilation to developed countries occurs in migrant-sending countries prior to any migration.

Temporary labor migration increases household income, allowing parents to purchase more schooling for their children and rely less on their paid and unpaid labor. Yet, migration involves extended absences of parents which detrimentally affect children, and its prevalence within households and communities increases the degree of "migration capital" available to first-time migrants. With a viable alternative to the domestic labor market for economic mobility, children contemplating future U.S. migration are less likely to invest in education. The shift in orientation from the domestic to international labor market has been the subject of my recent publications.

In September 1998, I began a postdoctoral fellowship at Z University. For my first year, I concentrated on publishing dissertation-related studies and developing a research agenda that exploits my multi-level and binational data. My ongoing and prospective research related to international migration focuses on the following topics:

1.　　**Impacts of migration on children's education.** I am extending my research on how migration affects the likelihood of leaving school by using multi-level modeling and additional data sets. I am currently comparing the relative impact of international migration prevalence at the family versus the community level on children's educational aspirations and educational attainment. A second project centers on how propensities to leave school have changed over time in response to the expansion of secondary education and historical phases of Mexico-U.S. migration. A third project involves matching migration data with detailed education histories that will allow me to conduct more nuanced event history analyses. A fourth project, in collaboration with Professor Name at the University of Wisconsin, compares the gender gap in returns to education for internal and international migrants. Research on Mexican labor markets suggests that men may possess advantages within Mexican labor markets that increase the propensity for educated women to migrate to the U.S.

2.　　**Permanent U.S. migration and children's education.** A logical extension of my dissertation research, for which I collected ethnographic data in California, is how the context of migrant reception affects children's education outcomes. This topic offers possibilities to rigorously test theories of assimilation and achievement within the blossoming literature on second generation immigrants. I would

B. G. Researcher, 2

like to use a nationally representative data set such as the NELS or AdHealth Survey to test competing theories on causes of high school dropouts among Latinos and other immigrant groups.

3.   International migration and social change. I have begun a collaborative project with the chair of the political science department at the Autonomous University of Zacatecas. In April, I will conduct two to three months of fieldwork in various parts of the state, collecting data on migration experience, social attitudes, and political behavior of household heads. Few studies use quantitative data and methods to examine how international migration affects non-economic life in developing countries. This research, combined with my dissertation, will allow me to produce a monograph on impacts of international migration in Mexican migrant-sending communities.

Recently, I have begun collaborating with Professor Name on issues of income inequality. This research is especially stimulating; I feel strongly about the topic, it relates to my dissertation, and it connects themes from my research during nine years as a graduate student at both X University and University of W. We apply relative distribution methods, an innovative analytic methodology developed by Professors Name and Name, to compare distributions of earnings over time between groups and assess whether changes result from median or composition shifts. I have begun two projects:

1.   The gender earnings gap during the 1990s. This study extends an analysis conducted by Professor Name that examined trends in the gender wage gap from 1967 to 1987. That research found that the recent shrinkage in the gap, the first in decades, was largely a function of declining men's wages. In the ten years since, the economy has undergone significant changes, many of which appear positive from news reports but which actually portend greater income inequality and a stagnant or growing wage gap between the sexes.

2.   The immigrant-native earnings gap, 1970-1990. This analysis, with Name of Florida State University, compares earnings of immigrants to those of natives, separately analyzing wages by race and gender. The issue is to what extent the declining economic progress of immigrants in the U.S. is a function of their individual characteristics—as some labor economists suggest—or a changing labor market context into which immigrants enter.

Sample Research Statement, Science

Research Summary - Daniel Researcher

The primary focus of our lab is to study the establishment of the germline using *Drosophila* as a model system. My project has involved the phenotypic and molecular characterization of a female-sterile mutant which was isolated during a P-element mutagenesis screen performed by Dr. Name and his colleagues while in the laboratory of Dr. Name.

My initial genetic characterization of the allele isolated by Dr. Name indicated that the phenotype was not associated with the P-element insertion on the chromosome. Excision of the P-element failed to revert the mutant phenotype to wild-type in 100% of the newly-derived revertant chromosomes. In addition, the P-element was recombined away from the mutation, confirming that the two were not genetically linked. Meiotic mapping with visible markers, followed by deficiency mapping, indicated that the mutation mapped to the cytological interval 24A3-4;24C3-5. I obtained several complementation groups and P-element insertion lines which map to this region, and tested them for the ability to complement our mutant. A complementation group that had been identified by Dr. Name and colleagues, named cutlet, failed to complement our mutant, which I have subsequently named cutlet[J1]. In addition, a P-element stock obtained from the Bloomington Stock Center, l(2)rJ865, failed to complement cutlet[J1], and I now refer to this as cutlet[P1].

Phenotypic analysis of the cutlet mutant alleles revealed defects in the development of several structures, including the eye, wing, and ovary. I have performed the majority of my phenotypic analysis using the eye because of the detail with which its development has been characterized. Histological sections indicated that cutlet mutant eyes were often missing photoreceptors when compared with wild-type eyes. Immunological staining of the eye imaginal disc primordia indicated that the photoreceptors missing in cutlet mutant eyes are the last to differentiate during normal eye development. In addition, cobalt sulfide staining of the pupal retina showed that structures which differentiate after the last photoreceptors are also underrepresented in cutlet mutant eyes. This suggested that proliferation may be affected in cutlet mutants. Indeed, BrdU incorporation in eye imaginal disc primordia showed that fewer cells were proliferating in cutlet mutants when compared with wild-type. The observation that a subset of adult structures, such as the eye, wing, and ovary, are affected in cutlet mutants, while others, such as the leg and abdomen, remain unaffected, suggests that there is a tissue-specific requirement for cutlet during *Drosophila* development for proper proliferation.

I utilized the P-element insertion in cutlet[P1] as a molecular tag to clone the gene encoding cutlet. Excision of the P element in cutlet[P1] reverted the mutant phenotype, indicating that the element was associated with the phenotype. I cloned the genomic region flanking the P element and used it to screen a *Drosophila* cDNA library, leading to the identification of a 2.1 kb partial cDNA. I obtained the 5' end of the cDNA by two rounds of 5' RACE. Sequence analysis revealed a putative open reading frame (ORF) of 993 amino acids with homology to the S. cerevisiae gene CHL12. CHL12 was isolated from yeast in a screen designed to identify factors involved in different aspects of the cell cycle. Both CHL12 and the 993 amino acid (ORF) have homology to all five subunits of replication factor C (RFC), a multiprotein complex required for DNA

Daniel Researcher, page 2

replication *in vitro* and in S. cerevisiae. To test whether this cDNA encoded the cutlet gene, I constructed two genomic rescue constructs. The first contained the entire genomic locus of the *Drosophila* CHL12 homologue, and the second consisted of the same genomic locus with an internal deletion which removed part of the coding region of the CHL12 homologue. I made transgenic flies containing each of these constructs and found that the rescue fragment containing the intact locus fully rescued the cutlet phenotypes, whereas the fragment with the internal deletion did not. This indicates that cutlet encodes the *Drosophila* homologue of CHL12.

To determine the mechanism by which cutlet affected cellular proliferation, I examined the ability of cutlet to genetically and physically interact with various factors involved in cell division. Since the cutlet gene product resembles replication factor C (RFC), I focused on factors involved in DNA replication as potential mediators of cutlet function. I examined the ability of cutlet to genetically and physically interact with proliferating cell nuclear antigen (PCNA), a factor that physically interacts with RFC and recruits DNA polymerase d to the primer-template junction and is required for DNA replication in vitro. Mutations in the *Drosophila* homologue of PCNA failed to dominantly enhance the cutlet mutant phenotype, and using a number of molecular and biochemical approaches, such as yeast two hybrid and GST pull-down assays, I was unable to detect a physical interaction between Cutlet and PCNA.

In addition to examining the ability of cutlet to interact with PCNA, I also investigated the possibility that cutlet interacts with the RFC complex directly. Mammalian RFC was originally isolated from tissue culture cell extracts, and each of the five subunits have been cloned. A cutlet homologue has never been found to purify with the RFC complex and is not required for DNA replication in vitro. I found that mutations in the *Drosophila* homologue of the 40 kD subunit of RFC (RFC40) dominantly enhance the cutlet mutant phenotype. Moreover, I have found that Cutlet can physically associate with RFC40 and the *Drosophila* homologue of the large subunit of RFC in a yeast two hybrid assay. I have mapped the regions of Cutlet involved in these interactions and found that they are in different parts of the Cutlet protein, suggesting that Cutlet has the ability to interact with both factors at the same time, and may form a complex with the RFC subunits. Interestingly, sequence analysis of the alleles of cutlet obtained from the Sokolowski lab has revealed two alleles with mutations in the region that interacts with RFC40. This further supports a model in which Cutlet physically associates and modifies RFC activity *in vivo*.

I am more precisely mapping the regions of Cutlet that interact with RFC40 and the large subunit of RFC, as well as examining whether the mutations identified in the RFC40-interaction domain of Cutlet disrupt the ability of Cutlet to associate with RFC40. To investigate the mechanism of the tissue-specific phenotypes seen in cutlet mutants, I have raised antibodies to the N-terminus of Cutlet. I have characterized these antibodies by Western analysis and immunohistochemistry, and am currently using them to examine the tissue and cellular distribution of Cutlet protein during development.

Sample Statement of Teaching Philosophy, Humanities

STATEMENT OF TEACHING PHILOSOPHY

Aaron Candidate

When I studied history in high school and most of college, it was a matter of names, dates, places, and "important" events. This was uninspiring, and it was not until late in my college career that I discovered that history can involve asking, and sometimes answering, questions about people's lives, about culture, about the difference between politics and policy, and about the origins of the present day. History is not about some disembodied past, but about the continual creation of a complex, but potentially comprehensible, world society. The relevance of that approach to history is something which I have always tried to communicate and instill in my students

Teaching history is a delicate balance of facts and skills, questions, ideas and arguments. Knowledge -- clearly a priority of history teaching -- must be more than mere information. Students should leave a course of history study with improved skills in analysis and communication, and with a sense of the important questions and themes of the historical discourse. I try to show, by explanation, by example, and with models, how historical questions are posed, contextualized, investigated and answers are rigorously and effectively argued. Because history is an innately inter-disciplinary endeavor, students are encouraged to draw inspiration from and develop skills in many fields, including literary, social, political, and economic analysis. The core skill of history, though is the discovery and analysis of appropriate primary sources, and direct engagement with sources is far more interesting, and ultimately convincing, than derivative arguments. I try to include primary texts, literary, political, and social, in teaching at all levels, and the careful evaluation of sources in discussions of secondary literature. The most basic function of scholarship, of any form of writing, is communication, so I try to create writing and discussion assignments which develop students' ability to communicate complicated concepts and narratives in the clearest, most convincing way.

Historical education is made more complicated when it involves unfamiliar cultures, but it is important that students gain an appreciation for both the complexity and the relevance of other cultures. History is a very powerful tool for cultural analysis and understanding if it is used to both explain and to go beyond common perceptions and stereotypes. In the case of Japan, students often bring preconceptions of rice paddies, silicon chips, samurai, geisha, kamikaze pilots, and businessmen, but placing each of these in historical context and perspective can leave students with a better sense of Japanese culture and history and open their minds to other questions and issues about Japan and its place in the world. Japan is not, as it is often portrayed, isolated or unique, nor is it explicable with simplistic themes and terms. All of these misperceptions, however, can be effectively corrected in historical studies and can even be used to illustrate problems of historiography and cultural history. Japanese history raises very important and interesting questions about the relationship between economic and social change, about the nature of power and authority, and about international relations, among others, and these questions can draw students into serious historical discourse.

My goal in teaching is that each and every student leave my classroom with a better grasp on the facts and the tools to better understand Japan, to understand and use historical methods, and to have a clearer sense of how the world has come to be as it is today.

Sample Statement of Teaching Philosophy, Engineering

A. R. Candidate
Teaching Philosophy and Interests

Teaching Philosophy

The concepts of my teaching philosophy have been acquired from those that have influenced me and from my own experience. The primary goal is to build students' confidence, both in themselves and in their knowledge of the subject matter. I believe that a student's ability to perform as an engineer is highly dependent on his/her confidence and courage to apply the knowledge that has been gained. Additionally, I believe it is absolutely necessary for the student to acquire a solid foundation in the basic sciences like mathematics and physics while he/she is in an undergraduate curriculum. There are several ways to accomplish this objective. For example:

- Focus on practical as well as theoretical understanding of the material rather than a polarized viewpoint of plan theory or practical understanding of the subject matter.
- Conduct laboratories involving experiments to "test out" the findings of the theoretical work.
- Assign class projects for the semester whereby each student or group of students is required to design a new experiment.
- Focus homework and exams on basic understanding of the material learned in the class to a variety of engineering problems.
- Determine students' level of knowledge gained from prerequisite course material.
- Show leadership and conviction in teaching demonstrated by being prepared for the lectures, available during scheduled office hours, grading exams and homeworks on time, and creating a healthy environment with the students.

Teaching Interests - *Undergraduate Level*

I have a very strong undergraduate education and over the years I have also taught undergraduate students at the University of X both as a teaching fellow and on a voluntary basis. I strongly believe in a thorough understanding of the undergraduate material as this sets up the stage for future research in the minds of young engineers. I would be very interested in teaching design, statics, strength of materials, kinematics, senior design, and engineering mathematics courses. I have a strong background in mathematics after having taken graduate mathematics courses at the University of X. I believe that this knowledge would be very useful in building a sound mathematical background for the undergraduates.

Teaching Interests - *Graduate Level*

As a graduate student, I had the opportunity to give talks in various areas of controls and robotics in my lab and the department. I'd strongly promote such activities as it gives an opportunity for the students to learn something that is not normally taught in the course curriculum. Additionally, these seminars serve as a good aid in developing student confidence in giving talks. My primary interests in graduate level teaching lie in the following areas:

- Advanced kinematics and robotics. This would involve introducing advanced mathematical techniques in the study of spatial rigid motion, screw theory, and topics in algebra like group theory and Lie algebras and applying this knowledge to robotics and spatial mechanism synthesis.

- Advanced dynamics. This would involve studying rigid body kinematics, types of constraints, Lagrangian and Hamiltonian principles, and an introduction to geometrical mechanics.

- Introduction to nonlinear control. This would involve studying nonlinear differential equations, concepts of stability, and differential geometric control methods.

- Introduction to differential geometry. This would be a basic course in mathematics exposing the students to modern approaches in control theory and mechanics. This would require an introduction to topics in topology, Riemannian geometry, group theory, and Lie algebras.

These represent general topics and I would be happy to teach more specific research topics according to the needs of the students and resources of the department.

Sample Statement of Teaching Philosophy, Science

Joy Successful-Applicant
Teaching Philosophy

When it comes to being good teachers, scientists really have an advantage over scholars in other disciplines. Why? The reason is simple: we are comfortable with trial and error and constant experimentation. This is not to say that teachers should fail to provide a sense of structure for their students. While upholding organization, they also need to find a dynamic equilibrium, always evaluating and fine-tuning their approaches to give students the greatest opportunities to learn and grow. In my opinion, teachers (and students alike) should never get too comfortable in their academic pursuits, but should challenge themselves regularly.

I formulated these and other views on teaching as a result of my own experiences both as student and teacher in the classroom and the laboratory. One important and practical principle which I learned from taking an exercise class (of all places!) is that teachers need to be in tune with students, and be aware of their responses. The fitness instructor who taught me this (little did he know) led the class each week as if we were bionic like he was. The pace was dangerous, in fact, and he always just laughed and enjoyed his reputation as "Mr. Speed." The instructor failed to see that the class could not keep up with his routine. This experience helped me to realize that as a teacher, I need to set an agenda and plan for my students, but they need to be adaptable. I am not suggesting that I must adjust myself to every whine and complaint, but that I need to be able to step back a bit, put myself in their shoes, and see if there is room for modification. In other words, I cannot teach in a vacuum.

Similarly, I believe that teachers need to begin a course by starting everyone on the same page and then providing a common intellectual space for students to develop from there. This is difficult, especially since many students come from different academic backgrounds and interests. I developed this belief during my experience as a teaching assistant where I taught General Biology laboratory to freshmen. I tried to begin the course by explaining that while many of them may have taken Biology in high school, we would be approaching this course from a more mature perspective, in that the focus would be on applying what they learned and addressing important biological questions. It was not enough to simply memorize. I found that this gave encouragement to those who were anxious about the course and motivated the others who thought they would surely ace the class.

During my experience teaching these freshmen, many who were pre-med students, I felt the temptation to teach them every last bit of X, Y, and Z amounts of material, so they would be suitably prepared for their future. However, after attending a conference on College and University teaching, and sharing these thoughts with others who had also struggled with the same issue, I realized an

Joy Successful-Applicant · 2

important distinction. I should not ask myself "what should I teach them?" but rather "what do I want them to learn?" Students who are given less material but who are taught to think critically and apply what they have learned are likely to be better off in the big picture. This idea of deciding what it is that is most important for students to learn has guided me in my present endeavor at X College. I am currently teaching a non-majors' biology course for Elementary Education majors, many of whom hated science in the past and came to me with looks of intense dread. What a challenge! But the real education for me has been to decide what basic concepts and applications I want them to learn so that they can go on and teach science to young children in their own classrooms. This experience has definitely helped me not to lose the forest for the trees, a problem that can befall a graduate student as she finishes up her thesis!

Besides teaching in the classroom, I believe participating in undergraduate research is an invaluable experience that benefits the student as well as the advisor. I have gotten a taste of this recently, as I have supervised a highly motivated undergraduate in my lab since late spring 1997. Jung has been learning how to design experiments to test mitochondrial functioning in *Toxoplasma gondii*. I have found that challenging Jung's interpretation of data, or asking him how he would proceed, has further strengthened my scientific abilities as well as his own. I feel that this experience has prepared me well for my future role as undergraduate mentor. Therefore, I am eager to continue my professional development and apply my interests to design feasible projects for undergraduates. I believe that teaching students real life examples of how to address scientific questions that they read about in textbooks is critical these days. Just as computer literacy is essential, exposure to research at the undergraduate level is a vital part of the curriculum.

Finally, on an interpersonal level, I feel that in my teacher-student interactions (which I enjoy a great deal), I try to embody the same values that are a part of any good relationship: trust, communication, and caring. I feel that students know that they can trust that I will provide them with a solid framework of knowledge and teach them to think critically so that they can address important biological issues and problems of the present age. I also uphold that communication is key to the teacher-student relationship. I often give students the opportunity at the middle of the semester to evaluate me so that I can be made aware of their feelings as the course is progressing. Through these and other approaches, I try to create an atmosphere in which students feel comfortable approaching me. I look at teaching, not as simply a job, but as a lifelong commitment to undergraduates. Because I care about my students and have their best interests in mind, I know that I will always be motivated to do the very best job that I can.

Chapter 12
Web Sites

As more and more people use the Internet as a primary means of finding information and communicating, some job candidates are constructing their own Web sites. This practice is spreading rapidly from technical to nontechnical fields. Job candidates who take the time to carefully construct professional sites report that potential employers are interested and impressed.

A typical site might begin with a homepage that links to: a vita, a statement of research interests, publications, sites one has prepared for courses or other professional purposes, other professional sites (such as those maintained by one's professional association), and, perhaps, sites reflecting personal interests. The vita is also typically linked. For example, one might be able to click on an advisor's name and find a document with an entire list of that person's publications, or click on the name of the degree-granting department and be linked to a graduate catalog or the department's recruitment materials.

For candidates in fields where visual materials are important, a Web site offers an outstanding opportunity to make it easy for an employer to view work, rather than dealing with cumbersome slides or portfolios. For example, candidates could provide a complete set of photographs of a portfolio, diagrams of molecular structures, patented drawings for a new mechanical device, a clip from a documentary video, CAD-generated perspective drawings of a new building, or archival photographs of the ritual objects analyzed in a dissertation.

Obviously preparing a good site can become quite timeconsuming and one is rarely required as part of an application. Since at this point a Web site will not substitute for any of the written materials you need to prepare, before you set out to construct one to use in your job search, decide how many people are likely to view it, how helpful it is likely to be to you, and, therefore, how elaborate you want to make it.

Constructing a Web Site

If you decide you want to take the time to construct a site, here are some things to consider:

- Browse through other people's sites for inspiration before you start to construct yours.
- Keep the site current. Make sure that all the links are to current addresses. If you find that the connection to a particular site is slow, you might want to put a warning to that effect on the menu, so that the reader's first attempt to use your page doesn't result in a frustrating wait.
- Remember that millions of people worldwide have the potential to view your site. Even though site pages are frequently used as expressions of personality, including humor only one's friends might find funny, don't include anything unless you want it to be seen by the chair of the search committee at your first-choice school!
- As with a vita or any other job-search materials, review your site carefully, making sure it is perfect.
- You may tailor a vita to specific applications. However, because of the universal access to your site, if you have more than one version of it, anyone who views one may also view the others. This form of presentation requires you to present a more uniform view of yourself.
- Make sure the menus have a clear and obvious sense of organization. If you include many links to other sites, group them in ways whose logic is immediately apparent to the reader.
- Give some thought to the danger of having materials "stolen" or otherwise misappropriated. It may not be advisable to put up any material you have not already published or given in a public forum. You also may have some concerns about the use of your ideas. For example, your statement of research interests may prove inspirational to someone in your field with whom you view yourself as competing. Add a copyright symbol and a phrase such as "Not to be copied or distributed without permission" to everything you post, unless you don't care if someone else uses it.

A Note About the Sample Web Sites That Follow

The following examples, generously volunteered by real scholars, are provided to give you an idea of some of the wide variety of ways in which a site may be designed. Since they are public documents, we have not changed the authors' names.

Sample Humanities Web Site

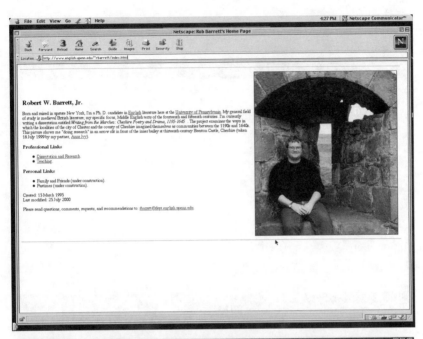

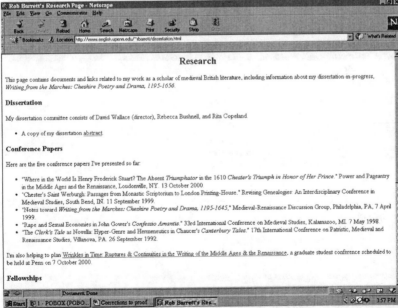

Sample Social Sciences Web Site

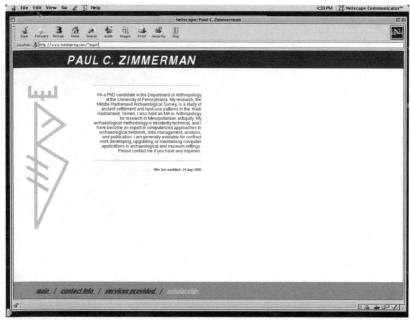

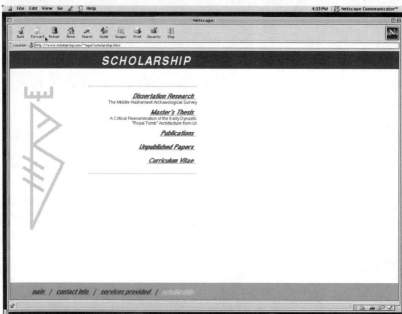

Sample Science Web Site
Author is an established researcher.

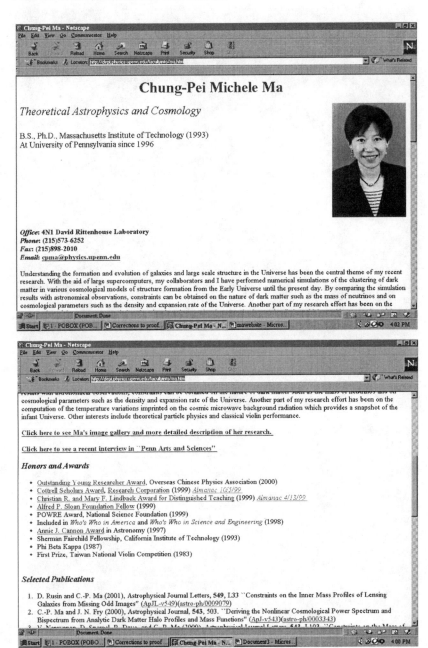

Sample Engineering Web Site

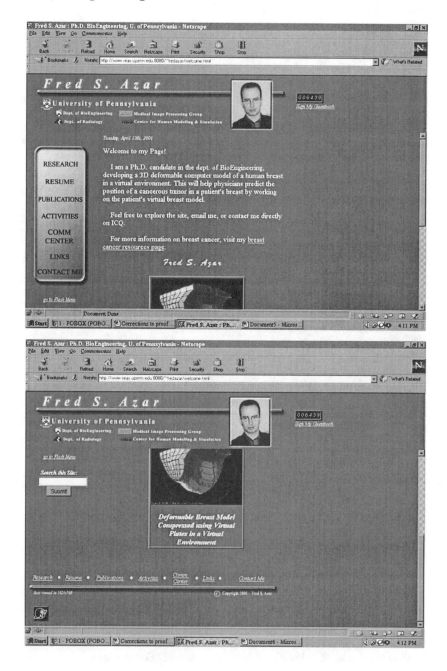

Sample Fine Arts Web Site

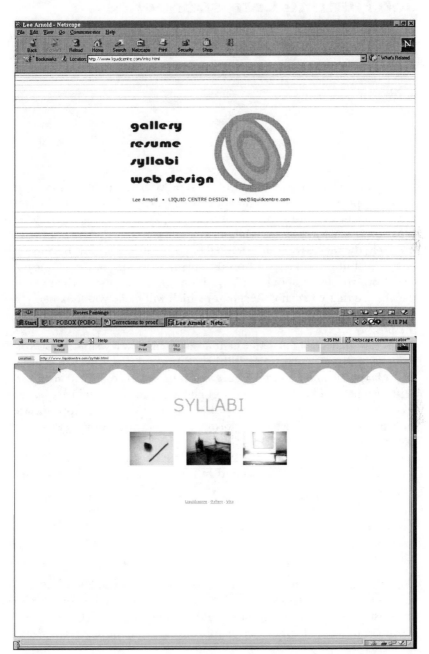

Chapter 13
Job Hunting Correspondence

Always include a cover letter when you send your vita to an employer. It is your opportunity to highlight your experience and expertise relevant to the specific institution and position.

Never send a form letter. Whether you will stress the potential of your research, the success of your teaching, or your enthusiasm for the mission of the institution will depend on the hiring priorities of the employer. The more you learn about the institution and department, the greater the chance that you can write a letter which will make you look like not only an outstanding candidate, but also one who will be a good "fit" for the position.

It is essential that your letter be interesting and well written. How you write, as well as what you say, will be scrutinized carefully. Use simple, direct language and no unnecessary words or sentences. If you are a foreign national and English is not your first language, have a native speaker read your drafts to ensure that the diction sounds natural. Appropriate language may be somewhat less formal than that you would use in your home country.

Proofread several times to be sure your spelling and grammar are perfect. Your letter should be printed in a readable typeface. Use a laser printer.

Cover Letters

Salutation

Use a formal title such as "Dr." or "Professor" even if you know the individual, because the letter normally will be read by many people. If an advertisement indicates that you should respond to "Search Committee," "Dear Committee Members" is an appropriate salutation.

First Paragraph

Explain why you are writing and indicate how you learned about the position, for example, "At the suggestion of Professor Jones . . ."; "I would like to apply for the position of Assistant Professor which was advertised in the January 6 issue of *The Chronicle of Higher Education*"; or "Thank you for taking time to speak with me yesterday about your unexpected need for a Visiting Lecturer."

Middle Paragraph(s)

This is the heart of your letter. Your vita describes your accomplishments up to the present. Your letter refers to these, but extends them into the future by demonstrating that you understand the requirements of the position and will be able to meet them. After reading your letter, ideally the search committee will be able to visualize you in the position and doing a great job.

Discuss how your achievements and qualifications relate to the specific requirements of this position. Let the department chair or search committee know what you have to offer without repeating your vita word for word. Explain your interest in the institution/position. In general, at a major research institution, it is most important to stress your interest in the research done by the members of the department; at a small college, it is also helpful to express an interest in the institution. If you are familiar with and enthusiastic about the kind of students a school attracts, say so.

One easy way to organize the heart of your letter is to use the structure of the ad. For instance, if the ad discusses four desired qualities and mentions two main responsibilities, explain that you have those four qualities and how they relate to successfully performing the two responsibilities. If you use this approach, be subtle enough that your letter doesn't sound mechanical. Don't abandon complex sentence structure in favor of bulleted phrases, as hiring committees often look at a cover letter as an indication of a candidate's ability to write.

Final Paragraph

Offer to provide extra materials or additional information or give the URL if they're posted to a Web site. Indicate how you can be reached and your availability for interviews at conferences or on campus. If you would be available for an interview at your own expense because you've already planned to travel to a particular location, mention that. Finally, thank the reader for consideration.

Letters in the humanities tend to be longer (up to two pages) than those in the sciences and social sciences (one page). Have your advisor and others read your early letters to make sure that you are expressing yourself appropriately for your field. If your campus career center offers services to doctoral students, counselors there may also be available to critique drafts.

Thank You Letters

Thank you letters are another important form of job-hunting correspondence. You should write one promptly any time anyone spends time talking with you about your job search, whether informally or in an interview. These letters can be brief and should be sent promptly after your meeting or interview. They can reiterate your enthusiasm for a position or convey information you neglected to mention during an interview. However, they should mainly express your appreciation of and interest in what was discussed during the meeting. If you have been regularly communicating with the hiring department by e-mail, it is appropriate to send a thank you that way. Otherwise take the time to use paper.

A Note About the Sample Letters That Follow

The following examples, nearly all generously volunteered by real candidates, are provided to give you an idea of what such letters look like. Other than to omit the names of individuals, we have tried to change them as little as possible. They should be regarded as excellent, but not necessarily perfect.

As you will see, they vary in style. Write your own letters in a style that both is appropriate to your field and feels natural to you.

Sample Cover Letter for an Advertised Faculty Position

Candidate's Address
Date

Name
Chair, Classics Search Committee
Excellent College
Address

Dear Professor Name:

I am writing in regard to the one-year Assistant Professor position advertised in the APA Positions list. I am currently a doctoral student in Classical Studies at the University of X, and fully expect to complete the requirements for my degree by this coming May.

Teaching has been an important part of my training at University of X, and I believe my background would be useful in your department. As a Benjamin Franklin Fellow, I have had considerable undergraduate teaching experience in several different types of classes, including first- and second-year Latin classes and recitation sections of the Classical Mythology class. The latter experience introduced me to the pleasures of leading class discussion and the challenges of transforming new material–some of it unfamiliar to me–into useful recitation sections each week. At University of X, I have attempted to recreate the inspirational classroom atmosphere I remember from my undergraduate years at much smaller institutions, Wesleyan University and College Year in Athens. Since my love of Classics began at a small college, I would relish the chance to contribute to that sort of environment at Excellent College.

I have been equally devoted to the research side of my graduate training. My dissertation, directed by Dr. Name, is entitled "Model Behavior: Generic Construction in Roman Satire." This study investigates the metaphorical language used to describe satire, and its implications for the poets' self-presentation. I argue that Horace, Persius, and Juvenal exploit the metaphors for satire that appear in their programmatic apologiae–satire as violence, as drama, and as legal process. Because these activities are also common subjects of satiric narrative, the narrative passages serve as generic markers and also reflect the satirists' attempt to construct their own poetic identities. Scenes featuring characters engaged in these acts–alter egos for the satirist figure–contain cryptic but very suggestive commentary on how satire came to be and what its important functions are.

With this research, I have been working to establish a place for myself in the scholarly community. In the past two years, I have delivered papers at regional meetings such as the Classical Association of Atlantic States, and at national meetings, including the American Philological Association. My most recent conference project was a collaborative effort; I helped to organize a panel on the satiric persona for the APA meeting in December.

Although my dissertation focuses on a single genre, it reflects interests of mine that I expect to resurface in teaching contexts in the future. One area that fascinates me is the place of ancient comic genres in the literary canon and cultural contexts of Classical antiquity. Comedy, satire, and related genres make excellent material for courses on ancient culture, and I would love to develop such a course at some point. Another special field of mine is ancient literary criticism, which I studied intensively for a Ph.D. exam on the ancient reception of Homer. Moreover, while both of these areas interest me in themselves, I believe that I can also parlay them into general civilization courses such as Excellent College's Freshman Humanities course.

I would enjoy discussing this position with you in the weeks to come. In the meantime, I am enclosing my Curriculum Vitae; letters of recommendation will arrive under separate cover. If you require any additional materials or information, I would be happy to supply it. Thank you for your consideration.

Sincerely,

Lily Scholar

Sample Cover Letter for an Advertised Faculty Position

Candidate's Address
Date

Spanish Search Committee
Department of Foreign Languages and Literatures
Large University
Address

To the Search Committee:

I am writing in response to your notice in the October *MLA Job Information List* for the position of Assistant Professor of Spanish. With the support of a Mellon fellowship, I am currently finishing my dissertation at the University of X under the direction of Professor Name, and anticipate graduating at the end of this academic year. Because of my extensive coursework and specialization in Latin American literature, my interest in interdisciplinary and cultural studies, and my commitment and success in teaching undergraduates, I feel that I would be an excellent candidate for the position you describe.

The position description indicates that you are seeking a specialist in Contemporary Latin American literature. Although I have a solid background in many areas of Latin American and Peninsular literature, my principal area of interest, as well as my recent research, has been in the field of twentieth-century Latin American literature and culture. My dissertation, entitled "Delinquency and Detection: The Neopoliciaco Genre in Cuba and Mexico," treats the detective novel after 1972, as both cultural construct and ideological tool in these dissimilar post-revolutionary societies. After analyzing the prevailing influence of Anglo-American models, the contributions of Borges and other Southern Cone writers, and the cross-influence of the Spanish neopoliciaco, I use criticism by Jameson, Sontag, Homi Bhabha, Luis Rogelio Nogueras, Carlos Monsivais and others to examine the mechanisms of control–and resistance–embedded in what has been termed a popular genre. Portions of the dissertation that I have presented at conferences have been well-received, and I anticipate developing the topic further after graduation. My other research interests include nineteenth- and twentieth-century travel literature, superstition in early twentieth-century Argentine literature, Regionalist narrative and contemporary Mexican literary movements. An undergraduate degree in Political Science, in addition to recent research trips to Mexico and Cuba, also contributes to my preparation as a teacher of contemporary Latin American literature and culture.

As my vita indicates, I have taught Spanish at all basic undergraduate levels in addition to serving as placement counselor for both French and Spanish. My preparation includes training in the ACTFL proficiency program and communicative language instruction, coursework in applied linguistics and pedagogy, and extensive research and design of computer-aided language learning (CALL) tools. Anonymous evaluations by my students over the years have been consistently enthusiastic, stressing my knowledge of the material, accessibility, and effectiveness in teaching. As a member of the academic community at the University of X, I currently serve as the faculty-student liaison for the Spanish Graduate Group, in addition to organizing last year's annual graduate colloquium and my ongoing work as assistant to the editors of the *Hispanic Review.*

I am committed to staying in the Delaware Valley area, and it would be quite easy for me to come to your campus for an interview should you decide to consider my application. I would also be glad to meet at the December MLA conference if that is convenient. My curriculum vitae is enclosed, with copies of my transcript and letters of recommendation to follow under separate cover. Because the position description stresses commitment to teaching, I am sending an additional letter of recommendation that specifically addresses my teaching skills. Please contact me if any further information is required. Thank you for your consideration. I look forward to hearing from you.

Sincerely,

A. S. Candidate

Sample Cover Letter for an Advertised Faculty Position
Position is a joint appointment.

Candidate's Address
Date

Professor Name, Search Committee Chair
c/o Ms. Name
Computer Science Department
Major Research University
Address

Dear Professor Name and Members of the Search Committee:

I am delighted to apply for Major Research University's joint faculty position in linguistics and computer science. Achieving breadth and depth in both these fields has been my consistent goal at the wonderfully interdisciplinary University of X, where I am currently completing my Ph.D. in computational linguistics. I publish regularly in both communities, have taken most of the course offerings of both departments at University of X, and am sensitive in my work to the concerns and methods of both disciplines. Your departments in linguistics and CS are top-notch; I would welcome the opportunity to continue my research and teaching among the excellent graduate students, undergraduates, and faculty there.

My dissertation concerns the representation and acquisition of lexicalized probabilistic grammars, which pay particular attention to the interplay of specific words. In previous work, particularly 1994 -1996, I showed that such grammars yielded 93% accuracy on the crucial task of parsing ambiguous, real-world text (*The Wall Street Journal*). I also sped up the associated parsing algorithm from $O(n^5)$ to $O(n^3)$. My dissertation expands probabilistic grammars to recognize, for the first time, their *transformational* structure. It shows how to *learn* that structure by generalizing automatically from a limited set of examples. The generalization technique uses a Bayesian graphical model that is motivated by long-standing concerns of linguistics.

My other major contribution has been in phonology. The new framework in linguistics (since 1993) is that pronunciations arise in part from the interaction of language-specific constraints. This begs the large linguistic question, "What kinds of constraints are possible in human language, and what representations do they constrain?" I have proposed a concrete, formal answer that is clean and well-supported by the linguistic data. Furthermore, I have proved several theorems about the formal power of the resulting system, designed and implemented exact algorithms for discrete optimization over the infinitely many possible pronunciations, and proved a lower bound on the complexity of such algorithms.

My other interests include the application of natural-language processing techniques to the Internet. All this work is described in the enclosed research statement. I am also sending sample course descriptions. You will find further research and evidence of successful teaching listed on my CV, and all my papers and abstracts are available at http://www.cs.ux.edu/ ~ name.

The following computational linguists have agreed to serve as references:
- Prof. Name, Computer Science and Linguistics, U. of X, name@x.edu
- Prof. Name, Linguistics and Computer Science, U. of X, name@x.edu
- Prof. Name, Linguistics, University of Y, name@y.edu
- Dr. Name, ABC Labs Research, name@abc.com
- Dr. Name, Major Microsystems Laboratories, name@mml.com

Thank you for your consideration.

Sincerely,

Jared Researcher

Sample Cover Letter for a Position on a Funded Research Project

Candidate's Address
Date

Dr. Name
Director
Educational Project
Address

Dear Dr. Name:

I am writing to apply for the position of Classroom Ethnographer. I am a doctoral candidate at the University of X, and I plan to defend my dissertation in June.

I have done extensive classroom observation in multiethnic, high-poverty, and urban public schools of Philadelphia in order to document educational reform interventions. My most recent project was working with a team of researchers from Research Consultants, Inc. and the Center for Research at the University of X, in which we documented a math and science initiative (XYZ Science Initiatives). The research involved observing cooperative learning techniques, the use of manipulatives, and critical thinking opportunities in primary, middle, and high school classrooms. As a research team, we engaged in numerous discussions about what these instructional practices looked like, in order to code our field notes in a useful, consistent way. From this and my other experiences of observing classroom instruction, I feel confident about documenting an intervention using cooperative learning in a substance abuse curriculum.

I am also comfortable working as part of a team and in sharing data with those closely involved in the implementation of an intervention. As part of XYZ Science Initiatives, I also served in the delicate task of the bridge between the research team and the program staff in the Philadelphia School District. I shared summaries of my observations from school visits, classrooms, and professional development workshops with the program staff, which they very much appreciated. I also helped the research team understand the situation at the School District of Philadelphia.

Please let me know if you would like to see artifacts of my work, such as field notes from classroom observations (perhaps of a lesson using cooperative learning techniques), or a completed report. As you will see from my resume, I have been involved in dissemination of findings through reports to funders as well as through presentations at academic conferences; much of that work has been collaborative.

Thank you for considering me for the position, and I look forward to hearing from you.

Sincerely,

Sherrie Candidate

Sample Cover Letter When No Position Has Been Advertised

Candidate's Address
Candidate's Phone number
Date

Dr. Name
Department of English
Eastern State College
Address

Dear Name:

I am currently completing my Ph.D. in Linguistics at the University of X. I expect to complete my thesis by August of 2001 and plan to move to the area at the end of August. Although I understand that there are currently no open faculty positions in the English Department at Eastern State College, I am very much interested in your department, and would like to take this opportunity to introduce myself to you.

While at the University of X, I developed, promoted and taught a course on English grammar and composition. I had sole responsibility for this course; I designed the curriculum, created all lectures, assignments and exams, and taught all sections of the class offered between May and August. With input from faculty on their vision of the course and input from the students on their interests, I developed a curriculum that is a strong combination of linguistic theory and traditional grammar and composition. Students learn not only the rules of grammar and guidelines for composition, but also the linguistic theory behind them; for instance, rather than just telling students to avoid dangling participles, we look at the syntactic structures that underlie participial phrases and the questions of pronoun reference that can arise. Once students understand what a dangling participle is and why it's problematic, they are better able to spot one in their own writing and correct it appropriately.

This course was very successful; during the time that I taught the class, interest in and enrollment for LING 010 increased significantly, and the course was even added to a small set of courses offered at an off-campus site for the University of X's continuing education program. Several of my students became Linguistics majors or minors as a result of my class, and many expressed relief at finally understanding how to improve their writing. My course evaluations have been consistently very positive, and one student even wrote an unsolicited letter of recommendation for my file.

I believe that adding a faculty member with a strong background in linguistics and language at Eastern State College would be of enormous benefit to your program. First, it is my experience that any student who learns how to analyze languages comes away with a better understanding of the language and the ability to use it more consciously and effectively. Second, linguistics is a rapidly growing field with close connections to many other fields, such as education, English language, foreign languages, ESL, cognitive science, computer science and psychology.

Undergraduate students who have taken courses in linguistics will have the benefit of a new perspective on language and the mind, and a stronger foundation with which to pursue jobs or graduate work in any of these related fields. By its very nature, linguistics, as the study of human language, is of great relevance to anyone interested in studying a language, teaching a language, or studying the mind. General linguistics courses should be an important part of the well-rounded liberal arts education that students receive at Eastern State College.

As a doctoral student at the University of X, which emphasizes a broad approach to linguistics and language, I have received a solid background in a large number of subfields, including phonology, historical linguistics, the history of Spanish, syntax, discourse, and child language acquisition. I have presented conference papers in several areas of linguistics, on such topics as Spanish stress, language acquisition, and the history of negation patterns in Spanish from the 12th to 17th centuries. I have also been involved in current linguistics research on the parsing of English sentences, pronunciation in English and Spanish, the Spanish verb system, and dialect variation in Spanish. I am therefore able to offer courses in a number of different linguistic areas, depending on the needs and interests of your department and the students. For instance, in addition to courses on English grammar, composition, and the history of English, I could offer courses on morphology and etymology, phonology and dialect variation, discourse structure, language acquisition, and comparative grammar.

Enclosed please find a copy of my CV, a statement of teaching philosophy, and a list of references. Letters of reference, copies of syllabi, writing samples, and other materials are available on request. I am in the area regularly and would be happy to meet with you at your convenience. I can be reached at the above address and phone number or at e-mail address.

Thank you for your consideration.

Sincerely,

Nell Aspirant

Sample E-mail Cover Letter for a Postdoctoral Research Position

Date

Dear Dr. Name,

I am writing to you as a candidate for a postdoctoral research position.

I am currently finishing my fourth year in the laboratory of Dr. Name in the Department of Genetics at the University of X School of Medicine. I anticipate finishing my graduate work in the beginning of 2001. Arranging my postdoctoral plans in advance will give me the flexibility to apply for several postdoctoral fellowships prior to starting in the lab.

The majority of my work in the Name lab has utilized the *Drosophila* eye as a system to analyze the defects associated with the particular mutant I have characterized (see attached Research Summary). During the course of this work I have developed an interest in the various developmental aspects of the *Drosophila* eye. I have read some of your work involving dock, as well as the utilization of the eye for neurodegenerative disease modeling. I find both of these areas very interesting, and would like to learn more about the various projects in your lab.

I have attached my curriculum vitae, research summary, and list of references as Word documents. I am also sending each separately as an ASCII message.

Thank you again for your consideration. I look forward to hearing from you.

Sincerely,

Daniel Researcher
Dr. Name's Lab
Address
Phone, E-mail address, fax

Attachments:

DResearcherCV.doc

DResearcherResSummary.doc

DResearcherReferences.doc

[Note that candidate's name appears in the name of each document, so the recipient can easily identify and file them. Files sent as ASCII messages should have similarly clear headings. Alternatively, they could simply be included in the same message as, and following, the cover letter.]

Sample Cover Letter for a Business Position

Candidate's Name
Candidate's Address
Candidate's E-mail Address

Date

Name
Large Consulting Company
Address

Dear Mr. Name:

John Name at the University of X's Center for Technology Transfer suggested that I contact you about career opportunities at Arthur Andersen. I have an advanced education in physics which has provided me with superior creative problem solving skills and analytic and conceptual abilities. I have also developed my communication and business skills through leadership roles in student government and an internship in technology transfer. Though my work in physics has certainly been challenging, I am now interested in similarly challenging work with more impact. I would like to bring my communication skills, creative problem solving ability and my extensive leadership experience to Large Consulting Company to provide measurable positive impact for Large Consulting Company's clients.

With my background in physics, I am certainly comfortable and knowledgable about technology. In fact, in my current internship at the University of X's Center for Technology Transfer, I analyze the commercial value of new technologies, and their market potential, and then market the technologies to target companies for possible licenses. My computer technical experience includes the design and implementation of the complete computer automation and data acquisition system for an x-ray scattering laboratory, and the re-engineering of the computer systems for my current laboratory.

This experience in technology may make me an ideal candidate for a position in the business consulting/information technology practice at Large Consulting Company. However, I would welcome the opportunity to discuss the possible fit between my skills and the needs of any position in your business consulting. I will call you in the next few days to see if we can arrange an interview.

Sincerely,

Vijay Applicant

Sample Thank You Letter Following an Interview

Applicant's Address
E-Mail Address
Date

Search Committee Chair Name
Department of Theater Arts
Selective College
Address

Dear Dr. Name,

Thank you for arranging such an excellent opportunity to become more familiar with your campus and department. I particularly appreciate your timing my visit so that I could see a student production. The enthusiasm of your students and the range and depth of the opportunities your department offers them are impressive. The visit confirmed both my interest in joining you and my belief that I would be able to make a contribution to the department that would be consonant with your current goals. I'll be following up on Dr. Name's suggestions about funding sources for expanding the curricular offerings in Asian theater.

I'm enclosing my travel receipts. As you know, I'll be in London until March 29, but I'll check my e-mail daily. Thank you again for the visit. Please convey my thanks to everyone who helped make my time on campus so stimulating and enjoyable.

Sincerely,

Hernando Applicant

Sample Acceptance Letter

Candidate's Address
Date

Professor Name
Department of Economics
University of R
University Address

Dear Professor Name,

As we discussed, I'm pleased to accept your offer of a position of Visiting Assistant Professor, as outlined in your letter of April 14, 2002.

I enjoyed my day on campus last month and will look forward to working with you and your colleagues in the coming year. The students I met when I was on campus impressed me with their degree of preparation and motivation, so working with them will be challenging and stimulating.

Ms. Name, at your suggestion, has already been in touch to give me some good leads on housing. Thank you both for your thoughtfulness.

I look forward to seeing you when I arrive on campus at the end of July.

Sincerely,

Yin Li Researcher

Sample Acceptance Letter
Letter summarizes negotiations for laboratory start-up.

Candidate's Address
Date

Dr. Name, Provost
Small (Religious) College
Address

Dear Dr. Name,

I am happy to accept your offer for the tenure-track position of Assistant Professor of Biology at a beginning salary of $40,000 (I successfully defended my thesis and will have the Ph.D. by May 2000). I am thankful for this opportunity and eager to serve God by my full-time mission in the Small College community.

Since this is an appropriate time, I would like to raise a few questions.

1. Thank you for the information regarding the medical coverage and benefits package. The base salary, as you mentioned in your letter (2/27/00), should be changed to $40,000 in the contract since I will have the Ph.D. before I begin my position. Also, I am presently covered under my husband's insurance plan. Is there a way to relieve Small College of the obligation to pay for my health insurance and instead use that money toward salary, moving expenses, research, etc.?

2. According to your letter (2/27), the date of my appointment is August 21, 2000 while the date on the letter from Dr. Name states August 1. Which is correct?

3. As we discussed in our last meeting, while my main interest is in teaching in the classroom, I am also interested in the prospect of allowing students at Small College the opportunity for small-scale biological research. Undergraduate research experience is almost as indispensable as computer-literacy is for students nowadays, as you know. Therefore, I have spent time discussing my ideas with Dr. Name and have come up with a request for several items to see this through:

Cell-biology lab for undergraduate research (involving the new lab space that will be created in the room adjoining the animal colony room). My research involves using cell-culture and pharmacological assays to investigate the effects of different agents on the intracellular replication of the protozoan parasite *Toxoplasma gondii*. I have many small projects feasible for undergraduates to do that will generate results. Dr. Name has a few pieces of equipment needed for some cell-culture work such as laminar flow hoods (to maintain sterile conditions). However, an essential item that I need to maintain my parasite and cell cultures is a CO_2 incubator, which costs approximately $5,300. Dr. Name has told me that he could benefit from this incubator as well because it would allow him to use mammalian cells (which I will obtain through my collaboration at the University of X) for different experiments in his Cell Biology course.

Another piece of equipment which is necessary for the long term is a small -70 degrees Celsius freezer (~$6,000) for storage of cells and parasites. Dr. Name has told me that he would also benefit from this freezer since the bacterial cells and some other materials he uses in Comparative Molecular Investigations must be stored at –70 degrees Celsius.

Other miscellaneous items (like a small refrigerator, clinical centrifuge, etc.) would be nice to purchase at some point after the essentials are taken care of. It would also be helpful to have $3,000 or as much as can be spared for the purchase of general reagents, plastic ware, etc. Fortunately, I will be collaborating with my thesis adviser at the University of X for several supplies, taking some of the burden from Small College.

I realize that the amount of financial support I am requesting may appear to be high, but I believe that not only will my students benefit (through application of my research in the classroom and through independent student research), but also Dr. Name and his students as well. Even biochemistry majors might be interested in getting this research experience. I believe that these measures can move the Biology department at Small College to the place it wants to be. Finally, I emphasize that the focus of this request is to further *student* research–if I want to do my own intensive research in the summers at the University of X I know that I can. I am not trying to create a University of X lab at Small College, but hope to give Small College students the tools so they can learn about how the scientific method is actually used and to inspire in students an appreciation that science reveals the majesty and greatness of God!

Thank you for meeting with me a second time and for your support and prayers during my decision-making process. I am so thankful to be officially joining the Small College family. Please keep me informed of answers to my questions. I would be happy to talk with you further if you have additional questions for me. Thanks again and God Bless.

Sincerely,

Joy G. Successful-Candidate

Sample Letter Declining an Offer

Candidate's Address
Date

Dean Name
School of Education
University of Z
University Address

Dear Dean Name,

As we discussed by phone, I must regretfully decline your offer of the position of Assistant Professor as I am accepting a position at the University of Q, where I will have a joint appointment with the Center for Educational Assessment.

While there are fewer people in my field of research at the University of Z, I nevertheless found this a very difficult decision because I so much enjoyed my meetings with you and your colleagues. I was impressed with the school's collective sense of direction, and with the faculty's extraordinary dedication both to its own students and to students in the broader community. I'm honored that you asked me to join you.

I thank you for your consideration and generosity in answering all my questions and hope that our paths will cross again in the future.

Sincerely,

Stacey Hire

Part IV
Conducting the Search

Chapter 14
Interviewing

The academic interviewing process may encompass three different types of events: the short half-hour to hour-long screening interview at an annual conference or convention which serves as the central job clearinghouse for a field, the phone interview, and the all-day or several-day interview on campus which may follow a successful conference interview. If you are invited to interview for a job as a result of your direct response to an advertisement, an all-day campus interview may well be the first and only stage in the interviewing process. If you interview a lot, you may experience everything from highly structured interactions in which all candidates are asked essentially the same questions, to interviews in which you, as the candidate, must provide all the structure.

While there are many similarities between kinds of interviews, each presents its own challenges. At a conference interview you have a very limited amount of time to stand out in a field of candidates, often under rushed and stressful conditions. In this setting you need to be prepared to present your qualifications succinctly and interestingly. An all-day campus visit is a far more complex event. It usually requires a presentation and involves more people, a greater variety of social situations, and more ambiguity.

Any sort of interview, however, is far more like ordinary professional conversations than different from them. Any time two people meet each other, they form an impression of each other. An interview differs only in that the evaluative dimension is more explicit. Whenever you encounter an unanticipated situation, do what you would ordinarily do in a professional setting, and it is likely that your impulse will be correct.

In ordinary conversation, if you are asked a question you do not understand, you ask for clarification, rather than panic. If you say something that produces a puzzled expression on your listener's face, you ask whether there is something you can clarify. If a question spontaneously occurs to you as a result of something the other person has said, you ask it. If you can't answer a question, you say so. All these responses are appropriate in an interview. Most interviewers are far more impressed by candidates who appear confident and candid than by those who appear to be trying to give the "right" answers. While you should always give the interviewer the opportunity to take the lead, many people who conduct interviews are far more comfortable if the candidate feels free to volunteer information and ask questions.

Areas You Will Need to Discuss

In any interview for a faculty position, be prepared to address these concerns: your dissertation, your teaching, your future research plans, and your interest in the organization to which you are applying. If you are interviewing for a research position, your research will be the main topic of conversation.

Your Dissertation/Postdoctoral Project

Be prepared to explain your work to the variety of people you may encounter in an interview, from world experts in your area of specialization through the person outside the department, such as a dean, whose work may have been in another discipline entirely. Practice particularly the way you will explain your work to those totally unfamiliar with its context. The effort you will need to make to be concise and to explain relevance in that case may well also improve your more technical presentation to experts in the field.

You could discuss your work for hours, but prepare to begin with a brief summary (about a paragraph long). It should leave the interviewer with the impression that he or she knows what you did (be clear); the work was interesting (speak with enthusiasm, and mention interesting findings or conclusions early in your discussion); the work was important (discuss how your work relates to other work and suggest areas for future exploration). Once you've captured this level of interest, further discussion becomes much easier.

Approach this discussion, not as a student seeking the approval of more senior faculty members, but as a colleague in the field who, in this case, is an authority. No one who is interviewing will know more about your dissertation than you do. Some candidates find that if they think of themselves as teaching about the subject of their dissertation, rather than merely reporting on it, their presentation becomes more confident, lively, and interesting.

Your Future Research Interests

It's imperative that you appear to have some! Merely saying that you plan to publish your dissertation isn't enough. You may be so immersed in it that it's hard to look beyond its completion. If so, set time aside to think about what you might do next. The effort will be worth your time. A candidate who says, "I haven't thought about that yet," when asked about research plans places himself or herself at an enormous disadvantage. Prepare to discuss your ideas at a convincing level of detail. Try to convey enough enthusiasm about your ideas that you will carry your audience along with your enthusiasm and interest.

If you will require external funding to do your research, be aware of probable funding sources. In some cases it may be impossible to continue your research without external funding. Even if such funding is not essential at the moment, your discussion of possible outside resources demonstrates that you are a candidate who is planning for future research needs. Many departments are under so much financial pressure that they may particularly welcome new faculty members who show promise of helping to support the department.

For positions at major research institutions, you will be expected to be able to tell the hiring committee your projected start-up costs. To do this credibly you need to have, in addition to a sound research proposal, a good estimate of what external funding will be available, and a budget for personnel, space, equipment, and materials the hiring institution will need to provide to get you started. Often candidates need to work harder to get adequate space than adequate budget.

Teaching

A hiring department's interest in this topic will vary, but most will have at least some degree of interest in what you do in front of a class. Before the interview, read through the department's course offerings in the catalog. Indicate which of the current courses you would be prepared to teach, as well as discussing any new courses you might offer in relation to the department's current offerings. Be prepared to discuss your approach to teaching and successful teaching experiences you have had, giving specific examples wherever possible. When you discuss a course, be able to suggest the text you might use. It is helpful to find out in advance what is currently in use in the department. Even if you would not plan to use the same text, it is neither necessary nor wise to disparage the current choice.

Don't forget that junior faculty members are often expected to carry a great deal of the introductory teaching load. If this isn't your great joy in life, you needn't pretend that it is, but try to convey the impression that you will do introductory teaching competently and with good humor. Make sure you are prepared to discuss using the computer in teaching and involving undergraduates in research, as you are likely to be asked about both topics.

Your Interest in the Institution

Major research universities may consider it obvious that you would like to work for them, and a small liberal arts college in a remote location may press you more on the topic of why you want the job. But your enthusiasm for the department and the job is always important. After all, the people who are interviewing you work there, and it is not flattering to them if you seem to find their jobs uninteresting. You usually need to convey interest most strongly at less prestigious universities and at four-year colleges of all descriptions. The latter tend to pride themselves on distinctive institutional personalities and to hire people they believe will fit in.

Research the department before the interview. When you are invited, it is appropriate to ask the person who calls you to send you materials that would give you information about the department and school. Read catalogs and college guides to learn about the school. The informal guides to college written for high school seniors are particularly useful in conveying the atmosphere of an institution. Use library indices, the Web, and databases to learn about the research of faculty members. Use word of mouth to find out how others view the school.

In general, departments are looking not only for a candidate with outstanding independent research potential, but also for an outstanding colleague who will enrich the department, not simply by being present, but also by interacting productively with others. Be prepared to talk knowledgeably about faculty members' research. Try to search out and explore in advance areas of potential collaboration with faculty in the department.

During the interview, you do not need to be insincere to convey enthusiasm. Just talk about what you do find attractive about the institution. If there are no reasons at all that it appeals to you, why are you interviewing there?

Illegal Interview Questions

It may be helpful to you to know that employers cannot lawfully ask you questions that lead to illegal discrimination on the basis of race, sex, age, religion, national origin, physical disability, or, in many states, sexual orientation. However, they may be asked anyway, particularly in social situations. Try to respond to such questions calmly, answering the concerns they raise without necessarily volunteering the information they request:

Question: Do you plan to have children?
Answer: I see that you're concerned about my commitment to this position. Let me tell you about my research plans for the next several years. I plan to pursue them, whatever other personal decisions I may make.

Question: Did you grow up speaking Spanish?
Answer: Are you interested in hiring a native speaker for this position?

Some illegal questions are asked out of ignorance; others are a mistaken way to try to get information about one issue by asking about another (a common example is asking about a spouse's job in order to determine how long you are likely to stay in a position). Try to react to them nonconfrontationally and to use them as another way to demonstrate your professionalism. Do not feel obligated, however, to provide information that you cannot legally be asked to give.

Question: What does your spouse do?
Answer: (If you feel that providing the information might work to your advantage.) We're fortunate that he's a systems consultant, and can work anywhere he has a telephone line.

If you are very uncomfortable with the direction a question is taking, you may politely ask the interviewer why that question is important and how it relates to the position you are seeking. This should alert the interviewer that you feel the question is inappropriate. Be aware, however, that there is some risk associated with this approach.

Question: Are you married?
Answer: Can you tell me how you feel that that would be important for the position we're discussing?

Sometimes it is to your advantage to volunteer information your interviewers may hesitate to request. The law can regulate what is viewed as appropriate to ask, but it does not eliminate employers' concerns, legitimate or not. For example, if you have a physical disability, your interviewers may appreciate it if you explain how you work with it. (If you do have a disability, be sure you are familiar with the protection afforded you by the Americans with Disabilities Act.) If you are much older than the average job candidate, it may be helpful to volunteer remarks that will give the impression that you can work comfortably with younger colleagues. Be alert to comments that may reveal a concern.

Comment: We were all impressed by the years you had spent in business before you got your Ph.D.

Response: Yes, I really enjoyed those years. I feel fortunate to have the opportunity to prove myself again in a new field. (Indirectly addresses concern that age and experience may make him or her unable to work comfortably in a junior position.)

Bizarre Interview Questions

Some questions, while not illegal, are inappropriate and weird. "What motto do you live by?" "What is the meaning of life?" "Tell us a joke." While you won't often be asked the likes of these, if you do a lot of interviewing, you may occasionally encounter one. In most cases the rest of the hiring committee will find the question as odd as you do. Try to respond cheerfully and matter-of-factly, but don't be constrained by the question. For example, if you can't think of a joke, say you enjoy laughing at other people's. Then, if you can, steer the conversation back to a more appropriate topic.

A Note About Attire

Wear something that conveys a professional appearance and won't detract attention from what you have to say. In general for both men and women this means something with a jacket. However, there is wide variation by field. In some cases a suit is virtually required and in others it is overkill. In some fields dressing with flair is an asset and in others a liability. Dress more casually for informal events that may be planned as part of an all-day visit. If you have the opportunity, watch what is worn by candidates who are interviewing with your own department. Also ask for advice from the best-dressed members of your department. Quality and professionalism are more important than variety. Invest in one good outfit and use changes of shirts or accessories to avoid being a rerun of yourself from one day to the next. Have a portfolio or briefcase, even if it is an inexpensive one, to keep track of papers and handouts.

When All Else Fails

It happens to nearly everyone. Nervousness about how you are doing in an interview interferes with showing yourself at your best. This is why some people interview better with departments they are less interested in. Your preparation for the interview should include enough sleep or exercise or whatever else lets you approach it in as relaxed a fashion as possible.

If you pay too much attention to "body language" during an interview, you will probably distract yourself from the points you are trying to address. However, be aware of how you tend to show nervousness (tapping feet, clasping hands, or whatever) and during the interview occasionally notice how you are behaving. If you are not sitting in a fairly open, relaxed position, change to one. Sitting with your arms crossed or holding your hands creates a closed, uncomfortable impression, and sitting more confidently will probably make you feel more confident as well. It's fine to gesture as you would in any other professional conversation. Holding your breath is a common nervous reaction that makes your speech choppy. Remember to breathe as you speak, and you will appear more relaxed.

Learn to use introductory "structuring" phrases which will let you buy time before trying to answer a question that throws you. They are better than twisting your hands or saying "um." For example:

- That's an interesting question. Let me take a moment to decide how best to respond to it.
- We need to consider several factors. First . . .
- I've never considered it from that point of view, but perhaps . . .
- I'd be glad to tell you about it.
- I'm sorry, but I'm not sure I understand your question. Do you mean . . .

You are expected to be somewhat nervous, but if you feel nervousness is getting in the way of expressing yourself clearly or is making your interviewers uncomfortable, it is best to make a direct reference to it. Paradoxically, the minute you admit you are nervous, you are likely to become less so, as well as to relax the interviewer. Examples of "defusing" statements might be:

- Excuse me for speaking so rapidly. I've been looking forward to the chance to speak with you.
- Excuse me, but let me take a second to collect my thoughts. I'm a little nervous, because I'm so interested in this opportunity.
- Let me begin this explanation again. I can see that I didn't express myself clearly.

Preparation

Advance preparation, of course, will let you approach interviews with less nervousness and even with some enjoyment. Learn enough about the institution to feel you have a basic understanding of its size, mission, selectivity, and student body. Know what courses and programs the department offers and the research interests of the faculty. If you can't find key information on the Web and in the library, feel free to get in touch with the department and ask for additional materials.

The end of this chapter includes a list of typical questions. Chapter 15, "Off-Site Interviews: Conference/Convention and Telephone Interviews," and Chapter 16, "Campus Interviews," have checklists for these interview situations.

While you certainly don't want to memorize your responses word for word, it is helpful before any interview to fix in your mind the main points you would like to make, given the probable interests of the employer. Prepared with the knowledge of what you wish to discuss, you can use even unexpected questions that come your way as an opportunity to discuss the ideas that you wish to convey.

Many departments or campus career services offer practice interview sessions. If yours does, plan to take advantage of the sessions. If it doesn't, try to organize one. Ask a faculty member to give you an individual interview. If you have access to videotape equipment, taping an interview will give you the clearest possible idea of how you come across. If you don't have access to video, you can still get a good idea of your responses by making an audiotape.

In addition, departments provide an excellent forum for delivering the presentation you plan to give at a campus interview. Take advantage of this opportunity, welcome feedback, and add final polish to your interview presentation.

Questions That Might Be Asked in an Academic Interview

About Research

- Why did you choose your dissertation topic?
- Can you tell us briefly what theoretical framework you used in developing your research?
- Of course you've read ____? (names an unfamiliar article/book related to your dissertation).
- If you were to begin it again, are there any changes you would make in your dissertation?

- In doing your research, why didn't you ____? (This question can take many forms. You are being asked to respond appropriately to an intellectual challenge to your work.)
- What contribution does your dissertation make to the field? Is it important?
- You realize that several members of this department tend to approach the subject from a very different perspective than does your advisor . . .
- Tell me about your dissertation (asked in a meeting with a dean who knows very little about your field).
- Why didn't you finish your dissertation sooner?
- I see you have very few publications . . .
- What are your research plans for the next two/five/ten years?
- What are your plans for applying for external funding over the next few years?
- When will you have sufficient preliminary data for a grant application?
- What facilities do you need to carry out your research plans?
- How do you see your research fitting in with the department?
- Who would you collaborate with?
- What kind of start-up package do you need? (This question applies primarily to people in fields where research requires expensive resources.)
- Do you have the permission of your mentor to take this work with you? (This question applies primarily to postdoctoral fellows applying for faculty positions.)

About Teaching

- Are you a good teacher?
- How do you feel about having to teach required courses?
- What is your approach to teaching introductory ____?
- How do you motivate students?
- How would you encourage students to major in our field?
- In your first semester you would be responsible for our course in ____. How would you structure it? What textbook would you use?
- Many of our students are probably (more/less academically talented; older/younger) than those you've become used to at your institution. How successful would you be with them?
- What is your teaching philosophy?
- If you could teach any course you wanted to, what would it be?
- Have you had any experience with the case study method?

- What do you think is the optimal balance between teaching and research?
- Have you had any experience with distance learning?
- How would you involve undergraduates in your research?
- Have you taught graduate or professional students?
- Have you supervised any graduate students, rotations, or research projects or taught specialized skills?

About Your Willingness to Participate in the Department and School

- Can you summarize the contribution you would make to our department?
- Are you willing to become involved in committee work?
- Why are you interested in our kind of school?
- What institutional issues particularly interest you?

About Your Career and Personal Choices

- If you have more than one job offer, how will you decide?
- How do you feel about living in a small college town like this in an isolated rural area?
- I can't imagine why a young person like you would want to go into this field . . .
- I understand your spouse is completing his/her Ph.D. What if you receive job offers in different locations? (This question is not legal in most contexts, but you should be prepared for it.)
- What do you do in your spare time?
- Who else is interviewing you?
- What will it take to persuade you to take this job?
- What kind of salary are you looking for?

Do You Have Any Questions for Us?

The right answer to this is always yes, or you risk appearing uninterested. Prepare some questions in advance, but, above all, ask questions that show a response to what you have learned from the interviewers and that are lively, rather than formulaic.

Questions about salary and benefits are not appropriate now. Wait until you are offered a job to ask about these matters.

Chapter 15
Off-Site Interviews: Conference/Convention and Telephone Interviews

Challenges of the Conference or Convention Interview

Conference interviews may be relatively unimportant in your field. In many disciplines, however, preliminary interviews for most of the entry-level jobs in the country are held at the annual meeting. You may be one of ten or more well-qualified candidates on a long interview schedule, interviewing under conditions of stress and possible confusion. So what do you do? First, reassure yourself that other job candidates face the same situation. Practice before the convention so that you can convey key information succinctly and make the most of limited time. Practice ensures that when the interview arrives you can relax and respond flexibly to interviewers, knowing that you're prepared for whatever arises.

Be prepared to be interviewed by a group. Three to six department members is a typical size, but the number varies. When you schedule your interview, ask the person who is arranging it how many people will probably interview you, so that you have some idea of what to expect. You may have interviews in hotel public areas set aside for that purpose. Some departments will have taken suites of rooms for interviewing. Others will interview in an ordinary hotel bedroom.

While you may be happy to interview with everyone who wants to talk to you, be realistic in scheduling interviews. Allow enough time to get from one location to another, bearing in mind that interviews may run behind schedule. Don't book yourself so tightly that you arrive late and disheveled to speak with the institution that is your first choice. Don't hesitate to reschedule an interview if you find that two are too close together.

Keeping Your Audience

Important as the job interview is to you, it may be less interesting to members of the interviewing team. They may be preoccupied with other aspects of the conference, be tired, and find that interviewing a long series of candidates is not their preferred occupation. Make every effort to be engaging! You are very likely to be asked to discuss your dissertation. Try hard to give a succinct introduction to your subject and to gauge your audience's immediate reaction, adding more or less detail as their responses suggest.

During each interview, try to introduce something that will make you memorable. This could be some striking aspect of your research, the fact that your advisor used to be a member of this department, the fact that you're trilingual, or anything else that will help people remember who you are. Even if one member of a group does nearly all the talking, address your responses to everyone and try to make eye contact with everyone in the room.

Dealing with Difficult Situations

At a convention you may encounter other situations that do not conform to a script for the perfect interview. There may be schedule confusion, department members may float in and out of the interview suite, or an interviewer may have had too much to drink. Anything you can do to appear unruffled will work to your advantage. Try not to let annoyance at an interviewer's behavior get the best of you.

Always feel free to act in a way that maintains your sense of personal dignity. If anything inappropriate occurs (for example, if an interviewer keeps pressing you to have a drink when you don't want one), realize that setting personal limits is appropriate and will serve you well in the long run: "Thanks, no. I'd like to begin to discuss the position you advertised."

In the extremely unlikely event that you find yourself in what you regard as an impossible interview, in which all your best efforts do not dissuade the interviewer from creating a humiliating situation, feel free to terminate the interview, as calmly as you can: "I'd like to discuss the position, but now doesn't seem to be a good time," or, "There doesn't seem to be a good match between our interests, so I won't take more of your time. Thanks for inviting me to the interview." In such a case check immediately with your advisor or someone else from your department who is attending the conference. If anything seriously inappropriate has occurred, it may be possible to arrange another interview under better conditions.

Usually, however, convention interviews are hectic but professional.

Try not to get annoyed at minor issues and to keep a sense of humor. Everyone else will be interviewing under the same stressful conditions, and things won't go perfectly for anyone.

A Desirable Dilemma: Early Offers

Occasionally, in fields in high demand, candidates have been receiving immediate invitations to campus interviews, or even job offers, as a result of convention interviewing. While most candidates long for just this sort of dilemma, and the attention can be flattering, try to keep a sense of perspective. You may feel you have little to lose by accepting another campus visit, but stop short of exhausting yourself by making numerous trips to places where you have no interest in working.

If you receive an offer before you feel you have had a reasonable chance to explore the market, express pleasure at having received it, but explain that you need more time to make up your mind, and negotiate for as long as you can before you need to make a final decision. Don't let the overtures affect your perspective to such an extent that you begin to seem arrogant, an attitude that can quickly alienate even those who were initially very enthusiastic about your candidacy.

Conference/Convention Interview Checklist

Before the Interview

Get all the details straight when you arrange for the interview:

- The logistics of arranging interviews vary from convention to convention. Find out from your own department how yours works.
- Clarify the time and place for each interview. If possible, find out how many people will interview you and learn and memorize their names.
- If interviews will be held at more than one hotel, make sure that you know how you will get from one to another, and how long it will take, so that your schedule is realistic. Seek help from your department here.
- If there is enough time before the interview, ask to have sent to you any materials that would help you learn more about the school and department.
- Make sure you have the name and phone number of the contact person in case you need to reach him or her before the meeting.

Learn about the institution, departments, and interviewers:

- You may have limited time for research, especially if you have many interviews scheduled. In the time available, try to learn something about every school and become fairly knowledgeable about the ones that interest you most. Much of what you need to know may be on the institution's Web site.
- The many readily available college guides written for high school seniors will give you a quick profile of the institution.
- Conduct Web and library searches for information on publications by department members.
- Ask everyone who might know something about the institution to discuss it.
- Learn whether the department stresses teaching or research and how it presents itself to the world.

Prepare for the interviews:

- Decide what you want to convey.
- Practice answering questions with a friend, a faculty member, or your campus career counselor.

Bring:

- Extra copies of your vita.
- Copies of your dissertation abstract and statement of research plans.
- Other materials you may wish to show, if time permits: syllabi, reprints, abstracts of articles. You will not necessarily distribute all of these, but you will be prepared with them should you need them.
- Whatever accessories or repair materials (buttons, glasses, or an extra pair of contact lenses) you might need, to avoid last-minute sartorial disasters.
- Don't check anything important through on the airplane. Bring all the essentials in carry-on luggage.

During the Interview

If possible, begin by shaking hands with the interviewer(s), even if you need to take the initiative to do so.

If schedule problems cause you to arrive late for an interview, apologize, and then try to forget it and begin on a calm note.

If you don't catch a name when you're introduced to someone, have it repeated, so that you know it.

Do your best, and concentrate on the conversation with the interviewers and the ideas you are trying to convey, rather than on how well you are "performing."

When your interview ends, briefly summarize your interest in the position and what you feel you could contribute to it. Keep it short.

If possible, shake hands with the interviewer(s) when you leave.

After the Interview

A timely, brief thank you note is a courtesy which can reinforce your interest in the position. It is normally not necessary to write to each person you have spoken with. A note to the person who was chair of the search committee is sufficient; in this note, you can ask the chair to convey your thanks to the others.

Some faculty members will find an e-mail thank you perfectly acceptable, or even preferable. Others will find a paper letter more respectful. Use your judgment based on impressions you've formed in the interview and on communication you've received from the department.

Challenges of the Telephone Interview

As budgets for interviewing candidates shrink, departments are increasingly doing a first round of telephone interviews before choosing candidates to invite for campus visits. These are not impromptu calls, but conversations scheduled in advance just as a face-to-face interview would be. They save you the trouble of dressing up in your best professional attire, but present you with the difficulty of establishing rapport with interviewer(s) without an opportunity to rely on visual cues. Often the interviews are arranged as conference calls, presenting you with the need to quickly learn to recognize different individuals based on their voices.

You should handle this conversation as you would any other interview, but it will be particularly important to be animated and expressive in your conversation, since the interviewers will know you only by your voice. One seasoned faculty interviewer has suggested smiling as you speak. Assuming the physical expression, even though the interviewers can't see it, will help you assume an appropriate tone of voice. Feel free to ask for more than a normal amount of feedback if it will help you get to know the people you are talking with. For instance, if someone asks you a question without identifying himself or herself, feel free to clarify the person's name. Taking notes as others speak may help you keep individuals straight.

Telephone Interview Checklist

Before the Interview

Get all the details straight when you arrange for the interview:

- Clarify the time for the interview. If possible, find out how many people will interview you and learn their names. Memorize them.
- If there is enough time before the interview, ask to have sent to you any materials or Web addresses that would help you learn more about the school and department.
- Make sure you have the name and phone number of the contact person in case you need to reach him or her before the interview.

Learn about the institution, departments, and interviewers:

- It is as important to prepare for a telephone interview as it is for any other kind. See the suggestions above for conference/convention interviews.

Prepare for the interview:

- Decide what you want to convey.
- Practice answering questions with a friend, a faculty member, or your campus career counselor.
- Send to the department copies of materials you might otherwise bring to an interview to discuss, if time permits, such as syllabi, reprints, abstracts of articles. You will not necessarily have time to discuss all of these, but you will be prepared with them should you need them.

Arrange for the logistics of the interview:

- Make sure you won't be interrupted during your interview, by your call-waiting, your children, or anything else.
- Collect and have near the phone copies of all the material you may wish to refer to during the interview.

During the Interview

If you don't catch a name when the interviewers are introduced, have it repeated, so that you know it. You may wish to jot down names and any other identifying information you are given; no one will see if you refer to these notes during the conversation.

Do your best, and concentrate on the conversation with the interviewers and the ideas you are trying to convey, rather than on how well you are "performing." However, since you won't have visual feedback, don't hesitate to ask if you are making yourself clear, if the interviewers would like to hear more about a given topic, or if they would like to move on to another subject.

When your interview ends, briefly summarize your interest in the position and what you feel you could contribute to it. Keep it short.

Since you can't shake hands with the interviewers, try to say good-bye to each individually, if there are few enough of them for this to be practical.

After the Interview

As after an in-person interview, send a brief thank you note.

Chapter 16
Campus Interviews

Challenges of the Campus Visit

By the time a department invites three to five candidates for an all-day visit, it has determined that all are in some sense competent. During the interview day the search committee tries to assess such intangibles as "potential," "fit," and "tenurability." On campus, it is as important to be prepared to be convincing and concise as it is at a conference. In addition, the abilities to respond flexibly to the requirements of unpredictable situations, to talk comfortably with others in informal, unstructured meetings, and to convey interest in the institution to which you're applying will help you land the job.

As institutions increasingly view tenure-track hires as major financial investments, campus visits for these positions have become longer, sometimes extending to three days. While the minimum requirements of a campus interview are usually a presentation to faculty and an interview with several faculty members, a visit might also involve teaching at least one class, one to several group faculty interviews, meetings with graduate and undergraduate students, several individual meetings, meals, a reception, and entertainment.

You may meet individuals ranging from a dean to a junior representing the departmental majors' club, from genuinely stimulating potential colleagues to the curmudgeon who makes it his or her business to ask all speakers to relate their presentations to the curmudgeon's own field of thirty-year-old research. Flexibility and a sense of humor will serve you well. Be prepared for potentially problematic aspects of the visit.

The Presentation and Its Question Session

The importance of an excellent seminar, also called a job talk, can hardly be overemphasized. An outstanding seminar can make up for many other shortcomings, but a poor seminar is seldom forgiven. The seminar is used as an opportunity to assess a candidate's research; how he or she handles questions and thinks on his or her feet; how he or she performs in the classroom; and even whether he or she has a sense of humor and a stage presence that suggest he or she will be successful at conferences, in the classroom, and in other professional forums. Pay particular attention to giving the context and motivation for your research. Within the first five minutes you should convince your audience that your work is important.

In the question period following a presentation, you may receive questions that leave you at a loss, point to a weakness in your work, or are challenging to the point of hostility. Stay calm and don't let yourself be put on the defensive. Be confident enough to admit that you don't know something. Respond to even unreasonable questions reasonably. Be prepared to venture reasonable hypotheses. Practice in advance how you might respond to even the most off-the-wall questions about your presentation.

The Teaching Demonstration

In many cases you will be asked either to teach an actual class or to give a teaching demonstration. This is particularly common at community colleges, but certainly not limited to them. When the interview is scheduled, find out who will be part of the teaching demonstration. If it will be students in an actual class, find out what they have been studying. If it will be a group of faculty and/or students convened to watch your demonstration, plan to treat those people exactly as you would if they were class members. Plan to stay close to the teaching style that works best for you. If you normally give dynamic lectures, don't use the campus visit to experiment with small group work. If you shine at creating class discussions, plan an interactive session. If the group is small enough and time permits, feel free to ask everyone to introduce themselves to you before you begin.

The Broken-Record Syndrome

You may meet many people throughout the day without having a very clear idea of who is critical to the decision to hire you. Simultaneously you may begin to tire of hearing yourself discuss the same subjects over and over. It's extremely important that you be enthusiastic about these topics with each new person that you meet. Everyone who meets you will want to form his or her own impression of you. So tell your story again to each new person with as much zest and interest as if it were for the first time.

Social Events

Social occasions are usually part of a day-long visit. Realize that they are also part of the screening process. Follow your hosts' lead in deciding how much to talk shop and how much to talk about topics of general interest. It is a good idea, however, to seize every reasonable opportunity to discuss your work and your field. You can also appropriately ask questions during these times. Your hosts will appreciate it if you make yourself good company: ask questions of others; initiate conversation; laugh at other people's jokes; and display an interest in the people you are with.

If you have no personal objection to doing so, drink if others do, but don't drink enough to affect your behavior. Alcohol and interviewing can be a risky combination. One compromise is to have a glass of what is offered, but to drink only part of it. Particularly beware of "confessional" impulses. However friendly your hosts, do not confide that you are here just for practice, that you can't wait to put distance between yourself and your advisor, or any other statement that later you are almost sure to regret having made.

It is easier to handle these occasions if you are very outgoing than if you are shy, but shy people can convey their interest and intelligence through active questioning and perceptive listening. You must push yourself to be an active participant in the occasion. It is better to risk some less-than-perfect remarks and come across as an individual rather than as a quiet, inoffensive presence, so bland that no one is sure what you are like or what you really think.

Your Opportunity to Learn About the Institution

Interviewing is a two-way process. Even as others are assessing your candidacy for the position, you have an opportunity to learn about the institution and to decide whether or not you want to work there. Both schools and departments have their own institutional cultures. You are most likely to thrive in a department and school in which there is a reasonable measure of fit between you and the others who work and study there. Take advantage of your time on campus to learn everything you can.

Location and Physical Setting

Gauge your own reaction to the appearance of the campus. Does it strike you as lively and inviting? Or do you feel that it is impersonal? In the middle of nowhere? Impossibly urban and congested? It's unlikely that you would choose a job entirely based on its physical setting and appearance, but it is important to be able to visualize yourself as at least reasonably comfortable going to work there every day. Look carefully at the physical plant itself, particularly the part of it where you would be working. Do offices and research facilities appear adequate? If laboratory or computer facilities are particularly important in your work, your hosts will be likely to offer you a tour or demonstration of them. If they do not, however, and such facilities are important to you, ask.

The Department

Probably the single most important thing you will learn on a campus visit is what the members of the department are like. These are the people with whom you will interact on a daily basis, who will be available for discussion of ideas, and who will ultimately evaluate your performance. Will you be glad to be part of this group? It is certainly important to keep an open mind and to remember that first impressions are necessarily somewhat superficial. Nevertheless, your reactions to these individuals are some of the most important data you can gather during your visit.

Pay attention to how people appear to relate to each other. Does the departmental atmosphere appear lively and collegial? Extremely hierarchical? Are there obvious divisions between competing factions? Do people appear enthusiastic about where they are and what they are doing, or is there a pervasive sense of cynicism and discouragement?

Students

If you are particularly interested in teaching and your visit does not include any planned meetings with students, ask faculty members to describe both students and classes. If your visit includes any free time, you may want to spend it at the student union or other campus gathering place. Listen to what students say to each other. Introduce yourself and ask them questions. Pick up copies of the student paper and of any other student-produced publications. They will give you a feel for current campus issues.

The Institution

At a university, probably you will feel you work in your department and your school more than at the institution as a whole. At a college you will probably feel that the college itself is your employer. When you visit, you will probably spend at least some time with someone who represents a unit larger than your prospective department. Use this as an opportunity to evaluate the role that the department plays in the broader picture. Is it strong and respected? Slowly eroding? The bright, brash new kid on the block?

As you learn throughout the day, feel free to comment positively on what you are learning. For example, if your first interview of the day is with someone who devotes a great deal of time to describing the school's excellent computer resources, in the next interview you can explain that you were impressed with them and go on to explain why these facilities would be particularly advantageous in your own research. If you notice an extremely collegial atmosphere throughout the day, and at the end of the day the chair asks what you think of the department, by all means say that you've observed a lively exchange of ideas and are very attracted by that kind of atmosphere. Hiring committees like to know that you have read their institution correctly and can picture yourself functioning well in it.

On-Campus Interview Checklist

Before the Interview

Get all the details straight when you arrange for the interview:

- Find out the length of the interview day and what meetings to expect during it.
- If you do not already have a complete job description, ask to have one sent to you.
- Will you be making a presentation? If so, on what? How long? To whom? How should it be delivered? What audiovisual or computer facilities will be available to you? If you want to use a particular kind of equipment, don't hesitate to inquire about it.
- Will you be expected to teach a class? If so, to whom? On what? What has been covered so far this semester? If you would like to use audiovisual materials, find out what equipment will be available.
- Confirm all travel arrangements. When planning travel, allow more than enough time to compensate for flight delays or traffic jams. Find out how reservations should be booked (if you need your tickets paid for in advance, try to negotiate that with the department). Save all receipts.
- Make sure you know the name of the person who has called you, where you are to arrive, how you will be met, the name of the person who will meet you, and all relevant phone numbers.
- If there is enough time before the interview, ask to have any materi-

als that would help you learn more about the school and department sent to you.

- If you encounter unavoidable delays while traveling to the interview, call as soon as you can and explain why you will be delayed.

Learn about the institution and faculty:

- Use Web sites. In addition to specific information, try to get a sense of the campus culture.
- If you are visiting an institution where sports are a major part of campus life, learn the names of the teams, both at the campus you are visiting and at your own institution, and how they are playing this year. Sports are sometimes used as icebreakers.
- Use Web and library searches for information on publications by members of the department. Try to learn the names of everyone in the department, so you can address them by name during your visit.
- Ask everyone who might know something about the institution to discuss it.

Practice:

- Practice your presentation.
- Time your talk to ensure that it's the right length.
- Develop a "cocktail party length" brief summary to give to those outside the department.
- Be sure your transparencies, handouts, and presentation software are ready in plenty of time. If you are planning a computer presentation, bring backup transparencies in case there's an unexpected computer glitch.

Bring:

- Extra copies of your vita.
- Copies of your dissertation abstract.
- Copies of your statement of research interests.
- More than enough handouts. Make sure they look good.
- Samples of syllabi for courses you designed, reprints, abstracts of articles. You will not necessarily distribute all of these during the day but you'll be prepared with them if you need them.
- Something to do during delays in traveling.
- Whatever you need (running clothes, escapist novels) if you'll be nervous the night before the interview.

- Don't check anything important through on the airplane. Bring all the essentials in carry-on luggage.

During the Interview

Remember that each new person you meet hasn't heard your story yet. Be prepared to tell it again and again with enthusiasm.

If the day includes social events, follow your hosts' leads in deciding how much to talk about professional, and how much about social, topics.

If you don't catch a name when you're introduced to someone, have it repeated, so that you know it. Shake hands when you meet someone.

Acknowledge everyone present in a group interview, and, if possible, say goodbye to people individually when you leave.

At the end of the day, find out when a decision will be made, and when you may call if you haven't heard anything. Find out if you should turn in receipts then or send them later.

After the Interview

Take care of any extra receipts.

Write a thank you note to the main person who arranged your day. You can ask that person to convey your thanks to others. Reiterate your interest in the position. It isn't necessary to write to everyone with whom you spoke.

Chapter 17
Job Offers, Negotiations, Acceptances, and Rejections

In a tight job market, candidates primarily worry about receiving any acceptable job offer. However, job offers produce their own challenges.

Once an offer is made, you may face a difficult decision about whether to accept it at all. If you are considering an offer, you may have to agree on a timetable for acceptance, decide on your first choice, negotiate with a first choice school when you have to meet a deadline for accepting another offer, negotiate salary or working conditions, and deal appropriately with schools that you accept and reject.

First, make sure that you really do have an offer. The department member who tells you confidentially that you're the committee's first choice or the chair who says that the department is virtually certain that funds will be approved are not offering positions, merely expressing optimism. A job offer becomes a real offer when a salary and term of appointment are attached to it and when someone has put it in writing. If you turn down a job in which a letter offers you a position and a salary in favor of one for which you've been told, "We're as good as certain that the funds will be available," know that you're taking a calculated risk.

Timetable for Accepting a Job Offer

Getting Final Information

When an offer is made is the time to get any additional information that you feel may be necessary to make a good decision. Now that the school is "selling," you can feel free to ask your most probing questions. Be prepared to ask them when you receive an offer, even if you need to schedule another time to talk more extensively. It is not a good idea to call the department again and again asking a different question each time.

Consider visiting the institution a second time to take the opportunity to ask all the questions you can think of about the prospective position and employer. Whether or not you visit, if the prospects for obtaining tenure were not clearly discussed at the campus interview, ask for more detail now. How many tenured and nontenured members does the department have? How many junior faculty members would come up for tenure at the same time you would? How many people have come up for tenure over the last several years? How many were recommended for tenure by the department? How many were granted it? What are the standards the department would expect you to meet in order to recommend it?

Other questions involve the conditions of the offer and the job itself. How many courses are you expected to teach? Will you have an opportunity to teach over the summer for additional compensation? Is there a possibility of released time for research in your first year on the job? What resources will be available to support your research?

If a spouse's or partner's job opportunities will be a major factor in your decision, ideally you have already given some indication of that in an earlier interview. Now, however, is the time to find out exactly what the department meant when you were told that "We should be able to find something attractive for him/her." Possibly you will want to arrange for a visit to the area by your partner, if you can persuade the employer to give you that long to reach a decision.

Perhaps you would like to talk to others in the department who were not available on the day that you visited. Perhaps you would like to talk to someone who can knowledgeably discuss local housing and public schools with you. Whatever it is that you feel you need to know, tell the person who makes you the offer so that arrangements can be made for you to obtain the information. Do, however, limit yourself to questions about things that seriously matter to you. If you ask endless questions about what appear to be trivial details, the department may begin to question its judgment in offering you the position.

Negotiating for Time to Consider

Naturally you would like to decide as late as possible, in order to ascertain what other offers you will receive, and the school that offers you a job would like you to accept as early as possible in order to close the search. These competing desires are reconciled through a process of negotiation in which you both agree when you will give the school a binding answer.

Generally this time is measured in weeks. It would be extremely unusual for a school to ask you to decide in less than a week and a two-week limit is more common. Extensions to several weeks are not uncommon, and extensions measured in months are very rare. Before you propose a time to make up your mind, ask the school how long it had planned to give you.

Schools will understand that you may want to see how you have fared in the market. However, if in your interview you have talked enthusiastically about why this school is your first choice, be careful that your behavior now doesn't throw your earlier protestations into doubt. In any case, convey enthusiasm for the offer at the same time as you ask for time to decide. You may take this job and will want to begin it on good terms with your new colleagues.

When Your First Choice Isn't Your First Offer

If you haven't yet had an interview with the school that is your first choice, it's doubtful that you would be able to receive an offer from it before you must accept or reject the job that you have been offered. If you are well into the search process with your first choice, however, it is worthwhile to see whether you can hasten their decision. Furthermore, the information that someone else has offered you a position tends to enhance your chances.

First negotiate with the school that has offered you the position for as long a decision period as it can give you. If you are willing to take a risk, you may be able to buy the most time by saying, "If you need an immediate answer, I'm afraid it's no." Since this answer may put the offer at risk, it's one you should not give lightly; however, if the school is very serious about getting you, this response does offer the greatest incentive for them to give you a longer time to decide. Then immediately contact your first choice to let them know that you have been offered another position and to ask them what their time frame is. This is most effective if you have already interviewed with them.

Negotiating

Whether or not you will be able to negotiate successfully for a salary higher than you are initially offered depends both upon your discipline and upon the institution with which you're negotiating. Even when the amount you could potentially negotiate is very small, however, it is worthwhile to raise the subject. First, be prepared by knowing appropriate salary ranges and their flexibility for this kind of position at this kind of institution. If possible, try to learn through informal channels how much flexibility the hiring department has to negotiate salary. If, in fact, the salary you are offered seems exceptionally high, you may be less inclined to negotiate than if it is low. If you decide to raise the question of salary or anything else substantive, the right time to do so is after you are offered the position, but well before the deadline for making a decision.

It is extremely important to conduct your negotiations verbally, usually over the phone, but occasionally in person, rather than by e-mail. Doing so helps preserve the good feeling with potential colleagues which is your working capital once an offer is extended.

Remember that in the period between the time a department offers you a position and the time you accept it, you are a "buyer," in the strongest position to ask for salary or any other special conditions, such as research support, that may be important to you. Make the most of this opportunity by not rushing into agreements you may later regret. You may well be offered a position by phone. If you do not feel comfortable negotiating on the spot, thank the person making the offer, make sure that you understand its basic dimensions, such as salary, and ask if you can get in touch shortly. In the next conversation you can raise any issues that you would like to negotiate and agree on a time by which you will make a decision.

If you decide that you want to try to negotiate a higher salary, what do you do? Begin by expressing enthusiasm for the job and asking whether the department has any flexibility on salary. Usually someone who is prepared to negotiate will answer, even if negatively, in a way that leaves a tiny opening. Note the difference between: "only in highly exceptional and rare cases," and "I'm sorry, but we follow an institution-wide, union-approved salary pay scale, and there's absolutely nothing we can do about this figure, no matter how interested we are in a candidate."

If you raise the question of salary, be prepared to answer the question, "How much did you have in mind?" Frequently an inquiry on your part will be answered with a response that the person offering you the job will speak with others. This is wonderful, because it gives you both a chance to think further. Take advantage of the opportunity to seek additional advice from faculty members about the figure you have been offered.

As you discuss salary, consider its long-term trajectory. Some well-known institutions pay less at the beginning, but more as faculty become more senior. Some institutions offer relatively small salary increases as faculty are promoted. It's fair to ask the hiring department to tell you the ratio between compensation for new and senior faculty.

Occasionally someone who cannot offer you more salary may be able to offer you other things (or perhaps there are other things that you want more than salary). These could include a reduced teaching load in your first year, special computer or laboratory facilities, funds for travel and summer research, assistance to a spouse who is looking for a job, extra relocation expenses, or something similar. Sometimes candidates successfully negotiate to defer starting a position for a semester or a year so that they can complete a dissertation or a research project or give birth and care for a new baby.

Sometimes nothing at all will be negotiable. Don't hesitate to raise an issue that interests you, but make sure throughout that you maintain a pleasant relationship with the department so that they will remain glad that they offered you the position.

The terms of the offer may change during negotiation. Be sure to have them put in writing so that there is a very clear understanding, and a record of that understanding, between you and the employer as to what has and has not been promised. This isn't simply a method of trying to pin down the chair. Rather it is a way to establish a very clear written record and ensure that you and the department have the same understanding when it comes to teaching load, research support, and so forth. Normally all these issues will be put in a letter by the chair. However, it's appropriate, if the chair doesn't do that for you, to say, for example, "I look forward to receiving a summary of all these terms in my offer letter." Or, "My offer letter did not include a summary of all the issues we discussed. Could you please provide that for me?"

Accepting and Rejecting Jobs

At some point you have to decide. Do so with the idea that your decision will be binding for this round of the market. Make your initial acceptance or rejection by phone, then follow up with a letter that confirms what you have said. In a letter of acceptance reaffirm any special conditions that were offered by the department. Once you have made an agreement, you are ethically, and perhaps legally, bound to appear for at least the first year of your appointment.

Once you've sent in your letter of acceptance, immediately get in touch with departments where you've been interviewed, withdraw from the search, and let them know where you'll be working. Begin to think of yourself as a member of the department and continue to stay in contact with its members until the time you arrive for work.

When you decline a position, do so very politely. Thank the department again for its offer, mention the positive attractions it held for you, and let the committee know where you will be going. Never burn any bridges. You never know when you will meet the chair or a faculty member from that department. You never know when the people you turn down may be able to influence the direction of your career. So always stay on good and polite terms with your colleagues in other departments, including departments that you have decided to reject.

Backing Out on a Job Acceptance

When you accept a job, do so with every intention of taking it. Occasionally situations arise in which a candidate accepts a job substantially inferior to another which he or she is offered shortly thereafter. Is it ever acceptable to renege on a job commitment? Some people would say no, and others would say that occasionally any reasonable person would do so. Ideally, if you find yourself in this predicament, you will be able to sidestep it by getting the second institution to defer your starting date by a year, so that you can keep your first commitment.

If that is not possible, and you feel the second job is by far the most desirable, then you need to examine your own values and anticipate possible reactions of other people and consequences if you back out on the first commitment. By all means discuss the issue with faculty members and administrators whom you respect.

If You Do Not Receive an Acceptable Offer on This Round

Some years the job market is better than others. If you are in a very specialized field and come on the market in a year when there are few openings and many outstanding candidates, it may be difficult to obtain a position. At times a candidate will reject the only academic offer he or she receives in a given year, deciding that it would not be wise to take it, whether for personal or for professional reasons. Many fine candidates obtain positions the second or third time they go on the market. If you know you will face a tight market, begin to formulate a "Plan B" even as you apply for academic positions.

In many cases the best use of your time may be whatever kind of work is most compatible with continuing your research (or finishing your dissertation). The demands of a one-year teaching position are not always conducive to research. On the other hand, if you are interested in a position that stresses teaching and have very little teaching experience, a temporary appointment could be an excellent way to strengthen your credentials.

If you interview for a position for which you think you are particularly well-qualified but are not offered the position, consider asking for some constructive feedback. This will work best if you do not seem to be questioning the department's decision. You will need to use your judgment as you listen to any suggestions, realizing that it is unlikely that anyone in the hiring department will share every aspect of the decision with you and that some departments will be reluctant to say anything at all. Try not to take what you hear personally, but, rather, try to incorporate any suggestions in your next interview opportunity. Above all, work closely with your advisor as you evaluate offers, make alternative plans, and learn from the interviewing process.

Of course you will be disappointed by rejections, but try not to let disappointment permeate your outlook. Discouragement can foster a vicious cycle in which you come across in your applications and interviews as cynical and bitter, leading to more rejections and more discouragement. As you are waiting to hear about one option, actively pursue others. If you are particularly hopeful about one job, while you are waiting to hear, plan exactly what you will do if you hear that you have not been selected. It's easy to feel that the application for a position was a waste of time if you are not selected for it. This is rarely true. Preparations for some applications will make other applications easier, the good impressions you've made will last, and the people you've met can become part of a lifelong professional network.

Recognize that job-hunting is stressful. Whether or not the immediate outcome is positive, it is also hard work. Whatever the immediate visible results of your efforts, plan to give yourself breaks from the search.

Chapter 18
Additional Considerations

Many of the conventions of academic job hunting developed when most academic disciplines had clear boundaries defined by traditional departmental lines and most candidates were American men whose spouses, if they had them, did not have careers. As research developments blur traditional disciplinary lines, as candidates in the American academic job market become increasingly diverse in cultural and international backgrounds, and as men and women are increasingly part of two-career couples, job candidates are often changing more rapidly than are the departments that will hire them. As has been discussed throughout, as a job candidate, it is best for you to stress the common professional interests and identity that you share with those who may hire you. Examples of this approach follow for four common situations: job candidates with interdisciplinary degrees, job candidates who are part of dual-career couples, job candidates who are foreign nationals, and older job candidates.

Interdisciplinary Areas

If you have an interdisciplinary degree, you have the advantage of being able to apply for jobs in more than one kind of department. On the other hand, when you read job announcements, you may notice with dismay that they frequently occur within the confines of departments defined by traditional disciplinary distinctions. At times you may face the problem of seeming "neither fish nor fowl" to a search committee.

If you are looking outside your field, learn the language of that field and use that language in your vita, cover letter, and interview. Disciplines have their own strong identities, and search committees in a related discipline won't consider you if they think you can't talk to them in their language. If at all possible, try to have a letter of recommendation from someone in each discipline in which you are applying.

In addition to those in your own discipline, join other scholarly associations so that you are current academically, as well as aware of job openings. Attend their conferences. To make sure you are aware of all possible openings, ask faculty and recent graduates in the disciplines that interest you for suggestions of places to look for job notices. For example, those in departments of American Studies may see appropriate jobs listed under English in *The Chronicle of Higher Education* or in the MLA job listings and under History in the *Chronicle* or in the job listings of the American Historical Association.

Dual-Career Couples

If you are part of a dual-career couple, before you go on the job market you and your partner need to articulate your goals so that you will be able to devise a search strategy that supports your personal and professional goals and answer potential employers' questions honestly and clearly. Colleges and universities, like other employers, realize that a candidate may be part of a dual-career couple. Very often if a department is serious about you, they will do what they can to assist your partner.

It's a good idea to talk to other couples and find out what has worked for them. Consider the following questions in terms of what is right for the two of you, not what you think an employer wants to hear.

- If one of you has fewer possibilities, perhaps because of being in a very small, specialized field, will that person find a job first, before the other one looks?
- Will you both go on the job market at the same time?
- Will you go only to the same geographic location as your partner?
- What will you do if you both get great job offers but they are on opposite sides of the country?

If you agree that you are willing to apply for and accept positions that are not in the same location, consider the following:

- Can you afford two residences, travel expenses, duplicate household furnishings, and large phone bills?
- Who will do the most commuting? How difficult is travel? A nonstop two-thousand-mile plane trip may be easier than a three-hundred-mile drive, especially in the snowbelt.
- How will frequent travel affect you?
- How good are you at getting along alone? Consider that it will be necessary to be both single and part of a couple at the same time.
- Will your department allow you to concentrate your teaching into two quarters and be away the third? Can you teach only two or three days

per week so as to have long weekends? (Don't ask for these privileges until after you have received an offer.)

It is usually a good idea to reach a joint decision about where both of you will search and within which geographic areas you are each free to act independently. Waiting to discuss these issues until you each have a wonderful job offer in locations thousands of miles apart sets you up for deciding who will "sacrifice" an offer. If the relationship is your priority, it may work out better to decide in advance on geographic locations in which you believe you can both find satisfying employment, whoever gets the first offer, and to concentrate your search on those areas.

If you are considering tenure-track positions, look beyond the first job for your partner to other opportunities. For example, if you are offered a tenure-track position by a university that arranges an attractive postdoctoral position for your partner, consider what you both will want to do after the postdoc has run its course. In general, dual-career couples will find greater opportunities in metropolitan areas, where it may be possible to change jobs without changing locations.

The fact remains that, given the national nature of the academic job market, it is extremely difficult for two academics to make career development their top priority while remaining married to each other. It is particularly difficult if both are in highly specialized areas with very few openings. Accepting at least short periods of geographic separation may help to make it possible, but separation in itself often puts a strain on a relationship. On the other hand, if one member of the couple is miserable because he or she doesn't have a job, and the other is miserable because he or she does, commuting may begin to look more attractive. Most people find they need to make a series of choices over the course of a career. The decision you make now will reflect your current priorities and may well be reevaluated as time goes on.

Once you have made your decisions, be very clear with your advisors about how you would prefer that they explain the situation. Be aware that a department wondering whether you will accept a job offer may well make a phone call to someone in your department to ask how your personal situation is likely to affect your acceptance. For example, your advisor might be asked if your husband would really be willing to move. While discrimination based on couple status or parenthood is not legal, unfortunately we can't say it never occurs. Employers may be as likely to call the person they know best in your department as they are to call your advisor, so it is generally to your advantage to have as many people as possible know that you are willing to commute, are committed to a particular geographic location, or whatever else is the case.

Decide at what stage to tell employers that there are two of you: before the interview, during the interview, or after the interview, well before any offer is made. If you will accept or reject an offer totally independently of opportunities for a partner, there is no particular need to discuss your partner's plans at any point of the negotiation. More commonly, however, your partner's reaction to the location of the position or success in finding a job for himself or herself in that location will be a factor in your decision.

In that case, it's difficult to decide when to ask about opportunities for a partner. If you ask too early, you may lead the employer to wonder whether you will be willing to accept the position and, hence, perhaps to give less weight to your candidacy. If you ask too late, particularly if you make it clear that you will not take the job unless your partner finds a suitable opportunity, you may lead the hiring department to feel as if you've suppressed important information. In addition, if your recommenders feel that they've gone out on a limb for you unnecessarily, they may be less willing to do so again, especially if you've turned down an extremely desirable position. You'll need to use your own judgment, which will be improved if you seek advice from advisors and colleagues whom you respect.

Your strategy will be affected by your partner's situation.

Ph.D. and Ph.D. in the Same Field

Job-sharing may be an option if you are willing to consider it. Hiring institutions, however, may be skeptical about the arrangement unless they have had previous successful experience with it. Before you pursue this option, make every effort to identify some people who have done it successfully, so that you can get some firsthand advice.

More commonly, you each want your own job. If there is any likelihood that you will actually be competing for the same positions, how you will handle the competition is something to consider. If you and your partner are applying to the same department, you may hope that no one will notice that you are attached to each other. Even if you have different names, that is unlikely, given the small-world nature of most academic disciplines. Thus it is also important to let those who are recommending you know how you plan to handle your searches so that they can help you reinforce that impression. A department that feels it would be "pitting husband and wife against each other" might end up interviewing neither.

Ph.D. and Ph.D. in Different Fields

At some point in the interview you will probably want to tell the search committee that your partner is also looking for a job and see if they will put in a word for him/her with the appropriate department at the institution. This practice is becoming increasingly common.

Ph.D. and Non-Ph.D.

When it appears to you that a search committee is seriously considering you for the job, you may wish to tell them about your partner and ask if they can offer any kind of placement assistance, such as names of people to contact. Certainly, if you want help for your partner, ask for assurances about it between the time you are offered a job and the time you accept it.

Nontraditional Couples

If you are part of an unmarried or same-sex couple, the same personal considerations will apply. You will also, however, have to consider employers' attitudes toward your relationship. In general, they will probably be willing to do somewhat less for an unmarried partner than for a married one. Whether to immediately put on the table the existence of a personal relationship of which some employers may not approve is a highly personal decision. If you decide it's something you wish to keep private, make sure that everyone who will recommend you understands that. On the other hand, some couples decide that, since they don't want jobs in which they must conceal their private lives, they will be as open about their relationship as they would choose to be if they were married. It may be helpful to talk with other couples in the same situation to find out what their experience has been and what they recommend.

Foreign Nationals Seeking U.S. Employment

First, think realistically about your long-term goals. If you want to work in the United States only for the duration of your practical training period, don't apply for tenure-track positions. Instead, concentrate on short-term appointments, which frequently will carry titles such as "Visiting Assistant Professor" or "Lecturer." They are less likely than are tenure-track positions to be nationally advertised, so it may be worthwhile to make direct inquiries of departments you would like to join.

Work Permission

If you would like to work in the United States indefinitely, you and the department that hires you will need to deal with the question of work permission. Generally this is not a great problem in academic hiring, since academic positions are likely to have very specialized qualifications; this will make it easier for a hiring department to demonstrate to the U.S. government that it needs you. In addition, most colleges and universities are familiar enough with the process of hiring foreign nationals that questions of work permission should not in and of themselves complicate your search.

However, a great deal of paperwork is involved. Work with the office on your campus that advises foreign students to see that you handle it correctly. If your goal is eventual permanent residency or U.S. citizenship, it is particularly important to see that each step of the process is handled correctly. You may wish to obtain your own legal counsel. If so, choose the lawyer carefully. Often the campus office that advises foreign students can advise you.

Cultural Differences in the Job Search

You have doubtless become aware of American ways of conducting a job search during your stay in the United States. However, when you begin to search for a permanent job you may need to behave in ways that still do not feel entirely appropriate to you. Remember that, however supportive your advisor may be, you, rather than your mentor, are expected to make the most effort on your own behalf. You are expected to show initiative during interviews and in meeting new people at conferences or all-day visits to campuses. In interviews, Americans expect that you will speak confidently about yourself and your successes. Making eye contact with even the most senior people will be seen as a sign of confidence rather than of disrespect.

Some of these differences may present challenges to you in preparing for interviews, but console yourself that many Americans do not find the process of job hunting easy either. If you come from a culture in which the assertiveness required in an American job search would appear rude, it is important for you to make a particular effort to talk confidently to others and to initiate conversation. You can do so with confidence that you will almost certainly appear polite.

English

Any institution, whether it emphasizes teaching or research, will probably pay considerable attention to your ability to both speak and write in English. Writing and speaking are just as important to research as they are to teaching. As hiring institutions increasingly demand excellent teaching, a strong command of spoken English is absolutely crucial. Your campus undoubtedly has resources for strengthening your English. If you have any doubt about your ability to be understood, take full advantage of these services.

If your written English is correct but not colloquial, have a native speaker read drafts of your cover letters. Hiring departments will assume that your written English is at least as good as, if not better than, your spoken English, so be sure cover letters are both correct and colloquial. Pay particular attention to the section on cover letter writing in this guide. American-style cover letters may be less formal than those you would write at home.

Older Candidates

In any search, there will be applicants who have gone from undergraduate to graduate work at breakneck speed, others for whom graduate study is a second or third career, and others whose graduate careers were interrupted for any number of reasons. As a result, the ages of applicants can vary widely. Those at the older end of the scale are often concerned about age discrimination.

Unfortunately, this is a realistic concern. However, some hiring departments may welcome the additional experience older candidates have accrued. Anyone who feels "too old" has to take care not to turn a realistic concern into a self-fulfilling prophecy. Since age discrimination is, in fact, illegal, it's helpful to be aware of your rights and of the possibility of seeking redress when you have evidence that they have been violated. However, at least initially, it's best to approach everyone in your search as if they will assess your candidacy fairly.

If you are trying to assume a faculty position after considerable related professional experience, try to publish in an appropriate scholarly venue and to get some recent teaching experience, even if you have to do the latter for next to no pay. It's important to realize that, in many fields, your previous nonacademic experience will not be a main factor in hiring. Present it on your vita in drastically condensed form.

As you interview, it's best to address an employer's potential concerns without saying you're doing so. If assuming a faculty position would require you to take a salary cut, you will need to convince hiring committees you're willing to do this. It's probably best to do so indirectly, by stressing your enthusiasm for the job. Make sure you're above average for your field in technological literacy, because the older you are, the more some employers may assume you're resistant to technology and reluctant to learn new things. To avoid "threatening" younger, less-experienced potential colleagues, stress that you're eager to learn from them.

Additional Concerns

Anything that makes you not a "typical" job candidate in your field may be a factor in your job search. Common concerns are gender, race or ethnicity, disability, and sexual orientation, but there may be others. For instance, if you've come from a working class family and obtain a Ph.D. in a field in which many of your colleagues come from upper middle class backgrounds, you may have a sense of "difference" at times. In general, it's easier to be a "standard" candidate than a "nontraditional" one, because you may appear to have less in common with the people who interview you. The implications of various "differences" are beyond the scope of this book. Here are a few suggestions which have general applicability:

- Talk as frankly as you can with your advisor about factors which may be of concern (legally or not) to potential employers. What does this person think might concern a hiring department, and what information can you volunteer to alleviate the concern?
- See whether your scholarly/professional association has a caucus, subcommittee, or task force which addresses these concerns and provides the opportunity for networking among those who share a common situation. Many specialized newsgroups and electronic lists serve the same function. If you make these connections, you'll have plenty of people to ask, "How did you handle this situation?"
- Make an even greater effort to find out what you may have in common with the people who will interview you. Stress those points of commonality. Make an effort to learn ahead of time about topics unfamiliar to you which may be used as icebreakers.
- These issues and others are frequently discussed in *The Chronicle of Higher Education,* another good reason to read it. There is a vast literature of advice for candidates who are minorities in just about any sense. Read other people's advice and experiences, avoiding the material which is merely enraging or depressing and seeking out that which you find helpful.
- In some cases there are laws which offer protection from discrimination in employment. Your campus affirmative action officer should be a good source of information. It's useful to know when you are protected by the law. However, it offers total protection only after a successful lawsuit, a major undertaking which can derail a career and should be undertaken only after great deliberation and extensive consultation. What you really need to be successful in your field are allies, rather than adversaries. Concentrate on building alliances.

Part V
After You Take the Job

Chapter 19
Starting the Job

You have received and accepted an offer. Whether it's at a place where you hope to stay or will only be for a year or two, advance preparation can help you make the most of the coming year. If you haven't already done so, complete your dissertation. It's very important to have it behind you so that you can devote your energy to your new teaching and research responsibilities. Set deadlines for yourself and finish it before classes begin.

Moving to Your New Job

The most important move you make to your new job is psychological. You are no longer a graduate student whose progress toward a degree is directed by your advisor. You are now a scholar, about to assume a job which is both demanding and unstructured. You'll have to teach your classes on a schedule, but you will have to devise your own schedule for accomplishing your research and any other professional goals. You will get little feedback unless you ask for it, and your progress will be formally evaluated at infrequent intervals. Therefore, you must serve as your own advisor from now on.

In most cases, you also leave the city where you did graduate work. Plan to move to your new institution one and a half to two months before school starts. That means you should start looking for a place to live in April or May. After you accept the job, contact the college or university housing office for information on faculty housing. If you are moving a family and need to consider a partner's job or school or day care for children, have the housing office recommend a realtor or relocation company that can help meet these needs. Get the names of a couple of recently hired people in your department and ask them for housing suggestions. Also ask for help with your partner's job hunt. Most institutions can provide some assistance here. Try to get moved in and settled in July.

Get to know your way around the campus and the town or city. Become familiar with public transportation and driving so you can determine the most efficient way for you to get to classes.

Getting Ready to Teach

While it's summer and things are more relaxed, get to know the staff and learn how the department works. Get your new e-mail account and Web site and find out where to get technical support on campus. Learn now how to get things photocopied; when to place materials on reserve; which departmental meetings you should attend and when they are held. See what your teaching schedule is and start to think about setting up office hours. What are office procedures and deadlines? How are books ordered from the bookstore? Visit and become familiar with the library and computer center. Before classes start and life becomes hectic, get a sense of the timetables. If the institution offers an orientation for new faculty, take advantage of it. It's a good opportunity to meet other new faculty.

The most important thing you can do to assure success in your new job is to establish good working relationships with your new colleagues. Try to get to know them, both senior and junior faculty. Set up some lunch or coffee dates and get advice. Ask them what they wished they had known when they started. Learn as much as you can about both formal structures such as classes and informal structures such as how information is passed on through the department. Discuss students' abilities and expected workloads so you can plan your classes accordingly. If it's likely that you will be teaching large classes, find out how many students must be in a course before it is assigned a teaching assistant.

Every department and school has its own history and its own way of doing things. Listen carefully to everything you are told, but be careful to form your own opinions. If you feel you are hearing only one side of a story, take care to learn the other. While you are still new, try to establish a comfortable basis for communication with everyone in the department. Some of the people who will influence your ability to be productive are not fellow faculty, but the staff people in your department and school. They include secretaries, librarians, business staff, janitors, computing center staff, and the people who staff laboratory facilities. These people can help you greatly or make your life miserable. You should value their contributions and get to know them.

Your Own Research

You will probably have very little time first semester to do your own work. Your time will fill up with departmental responsibilities as well as teaching. However, you can base some of your courses on your own research and, possibly, teach your dissertation for your first graduate-level course.

Try to keep thinking about your research even when you can't really work on it. Do you want to continue with your prior research plans, or do you feel you're in a dead-end area of research and need to use publication as your opportunity to redefine your work? Try to have one day or a half day a week away from the office for your own work. If you are used to working closely with your advisor, you may miss the stimulus of that interaction, as well as the structure imposed when you work with someone else.

Of course, you will want to keep in touch with your advisor, but start thinking about others with whom you wish to collaborate or with whom you wish to discuss your ideas. Giving a talk on campus can give you useful feedback and help you make yourself known to people with similar research interests. You can use deadlines for calls for papers as a way of giving yourself a realistic schedule for your work. If no one but you knows or cares about your research and you face no deadlines, you risk putting day-to-day demands ahead of the more major goals you wish to accomplish.

If you are a scientist or engineer, your major initial task will be setting up your lab. You may need not only to order and assemble equipment, but also to recruit the people who will work for you on your research project. Your institution may or may not be proactive in helping with this project. Avoid future problems by taking the initiative to learn all the regulations with which you'll need to comply. Meet the people responsible for administering your grant. If you're doing something for the first time and know someone, at your new institution or anywhere else, who has already been through the process, save yourself time by consulting with that person. If this is the first time you've supervised people, spend time learning how to do that effectively, as well.

Teaching

You will have to make policies for your students and stick to them. Before questions arise, think about how you are going to keep order. Are you going to grant extensions and under what circumstances? How will you grade work? What are guidelines for grading in the department? Talk with other faculty and get suggestions.

Be as organized a teacher as possible. Do your lecture notes in whatever style best suits you. Keep your notes from year to year. Write them on a computer so you can both easily change them and keep them. Avoid teaching new courses in the spring. Instead, offer new subjects in the fall when you will have had the summer to prepare.

You may be given a big class that no one else wants, such as a survey or introductory course. Try to put your personal stamp on it and make it your own, yet, at the same time, don't feel you have to know everything. If you haven't had much experience preparing lectures, talk with some of your new colleagues or some of your former professors from your graduate institution. Find out if your institution offers any teaching help to new professors such as videotaping and teaching centers.

Students

In addition to developing your teaching style, think about your students. In many institutions they are seventeen to twenty-two years old and come with problems that go with that age. They are involved in themselves: trying to figure out who they are, academically, socially, politically, and personally. Academic matters are not their only concern. You may also have older students in your class whose lives and goals are quite different from those of the younger, traditional students. Develop an approach that will reach these students.

Self-Evaluation

At the end of the first year evaluate your teaching and consider your own observations as well as those of other faculty and students. Decide what you want to do differently and incorporate those changes as you begin planning for the second year. Get an informal discussion group going with other junior faculty and share ideas on successful teaching.

Keeping Lines of Communication Open

It is important that you get involved in the life of your department and take on some responsibilities that feel important, such as directing honors students, supervising independent study, freshman advising, or running the colloquium series. Choose carefully a few responsibilities and do them really well. Then you can say no to other things including university service. Try not to get involved in university committees during your first few years so you can concentrate on teaching and research. You'll have a better idea of where you want to concentrate your energy once you've had a chance to settle in.

You can strongly influence your new department's view of you. Establish an interesting, positive, and comfortable way of discussing your own work and teaching, speak up about the kinds of achievements you wish people to associate with you, and take an informed interest in what other people are doing. Try to develop a relationship with a senior professor who can help you out as you feel your way through the first year. Ask him or her to visit one of your classes and then give you feedback. Also find out how your colleagues perceive you. Are you seen as fitting into the department? Are you seen as carrying your load? Are you seen as productive? As an assistant professor you are entitled to regular discussions with the chair and senior people as to how you are doing. Such regular feedback will help you keep on track in the process of obtaining tenure.

It's also important to continue to maintain networks beyond your new department. Get to know other parts of your school or university and stay deeply involved with national and international networks in your own discipline. This involvement will help you stay aware of trends and keep you flexible in developing your own work. Since you'll never have enough time to do everything that might be desirable to do in your new job, frequently take a break to review your priorities. We hope these include "having a life," taking care of yourself, staying involved with family and friends, and other personal interests.

Special Considerations for Non-Tenure-Track Positions

If the position you have taken is on a nonrenewable contract and you will go on the job market again soon, it's especially important to stay in touch with everyone in your network. You need to plan your time extremely carefully, to balance your teaching and research with the demands of your job search. Do everything you can to protect your time, limiting your office hours and turning down all but unavoidable committee assignments. You will be tempted to focus on your teaching and your job search and to do no research. However, research may be what helps you get another job, so build in regular time to work on it.

Chapter 20
Knowing About and Getting Tenure

Most institutions have some form of tenure. When you interviewed for your job or during the acceptance discussion, you probably asked some questions about tenure at your new institution. Before you begin working, it's helpful to know how many junior faculty are granted tenure, both within your department and university-wide. If 80 percent of the faculty in the whole school are tenured, the possibility for tenure for new Ph.D.s is limited.

The movement for the tenure system began in the early 1900s and became very strong after World War I. It was developed to provide faculty with freedom of expression. Proponents of tenure believe it is healthy for the nation to have a body of individuals who can say what they want and be protected. Opponents of tenure believe it protects the incompetent and reduces institutional flexibility.

The tenure system allows the new assistant professor a chance to grow comfortable with the institution, with teaching, and with research. It allows the institution an opportunity to evaluate his or her work. The usual span of time before making the tenure decision is six years, with tenure granted or denied by the seventh. Some places, however, go eight or nine years before making the decision.

Criteria used to determine tenure also vary from place to place. At a major research institution, research publications are most important. Quality, not quantity, is the issue. Usually at least one book and some articles in refereed publications are necessary in the humanities and social sciences, while several journal articles are crucial in the sciences. The department may count only certain journals, so be sure to know which are considered important. Often, particularly in the sciences and engineering, much of your success will be determined by your effectiveness in raising funds to support your research. Concentrate on research, publication, and teaching—in that order.

At a small liberal arts college, while teaching is the most significant criterion, research has increased in significance. At such a school you should refine your teaching skills and develop your own personal teaching style that is well received by students and ensures that they learn.

At a community college, once one has taken a permanent position, tenure usually takes on more the quality of a natural step. While there is usually some review process, it is less demanding than at most four-year institutions and the default presumption is that candidates will be awarded tenure. However, it's important to learn the process and requirements at the time you accept a community college position.

Example of the Tenure Process at a Large Research Institution

The tenure process is different in each institution, and it is important that you learn early what the process is for you. The following illustrates the process at one large research institution.

Appointments

Appointments for assistant professors are made for three or four years, to be renewed for three years. Review for promotion usually comes up after six years and is quite lengthy and complicated. Less common is a ten-year tenure track, in which case the decision is made in the ninth year.

The Review Process

At the beginning of the sixth year, the review process begins in the department with the appointment of a three-to-four person subcommittee (all tenured faculty). The committee collects publications and teaching records from the candidate as well as oral and written recommendations from inside and outside the university. After these items are reviewed, the department has a meeting to take a formal vote.

Letters of support from outside the institution are very important. The department puts together a list of outside reviewers who are prominent in the field. You may be asked to suggest additional reviewers. This list is vetted at the dean's level and later at the provost's.

If the departmental vote is favorable, the chair writes a letter that includes the majority and minority opinions, adds his or her own opinion, and sends the letter with the review materials to the dean.

The dean refers the packet of material to a personnel committee composed of tenured faculty. This committee has three subcommittees: humanities, social sciences, and natural sciences. The subcommittee reads everything and makes recommendations to the committee as a whole. If this committee includes a member of the candidate's department, he or she will not participate in the discussion and will not vote but will answer questions. The chief job of this committee is to look at outside letters to see if the research is judged important. When the committee has voted, the dean writes a letter and sends the results on to the provost.

The provost gives the materials to a committee consisting of deans and other senior administrators. This group reads the outside letters and examines the financial base for the position, since most tenure decisions involve millions of dollars over a period of time. After a vote is taken, the materials go to the president.

The president reviews the files and usually accepts the provost's decision. The president takes the decision to the trustees, who act formally and legally on the case. A letter from the trustees comes to the successful candidate a few months after the decision.

The process can take months because it takes a long time to get the outside letters. At some large institutions the provost asks each school to bring up all its cases at once. Therefore the slowest department controls the process.

Example of the Tenure Process at a Small Teaching College

At one small private college where the emphasis is on excellent teaching, the tenure process is somewhat different.

There are three evaluations before tenure. The first is after two years and results in the dismissal only of candidates viewed as "hiring mistakes." The second is held in the fourth year and is becoming less pro forma. The third is for making the tenure decision and is held at the beginning of the sixth year.

The three criteria for all evaluations, including those for full professors, are: teaching, professional development, and collegiate citizenship. Teaching is the most important. Professional development, which includes publications, has become increasingly important, whereas it used to be equal in importance to collegiate citizenship. Collegiate citizenship is mainly committee work but also includes recruiting students, alumni activities, and advising some student organizations.

All faculty are invited to visit the candidate's classes and write letters of recommendation. However, recommendations from the candidate's departmental colleagues matter the most, with those of tenured faculty carrying the most weight. The candidate and department chair come up with a list of other persons from whom letters are requested. These include scholars at other institutions, students, and recent alumni. A dossier of letters is sent to the provost who makes a recommendation to the president by a certain date. The formal power for granting tenure then lies with the board of trustees who meet near the end of the academic year. The candidate learns the result immediately.

Advice

The years until tenure consideration will be the toughest in your academic life. Concentrate on research and teaching. Try to avoid being department chair or serving on many committees until you have tenure, unless you know for sure that your institution weighs such service heavily in tenure decisions. If you are the only woman or minority person in your department, your presence on all kinds of committees will be sought. Learn to say no to most requests. Know the tenure criteria well before you have to provide documentation that you have fulfilled them. At many institutions, teaching records are important. Letters are requested from students and recent graduates. Save teaching recommendations and start building that file early.

Seek regular feedback about your progress from senior faculty members whose judgment you trust. Listen seriously to this feedback. Make an effort to talk with faculty in the department to let them know what you are doing. Talk with colleagues about your teaching and about good classes so that they perceive you as a strong teacher. Remain in touch with those in the field at other institutions in case you need external referees. Send them drafts of papers, solicit their advice, meet them at conferences.

Usually the candidate knows at what stage of the review process he or she is. How strongly does your department support you? If it begins to look increasingly unlikely that you will be awarded tenure, you may want to start looking at other jobs before the formal evaluation process begins. Also consider the likelihood of tenure from an institutional perspective. How stable is the institution's financial condition? How is your department regarded?

Try to keep the whole process in perspective. Tenure decisions ultimately involve many variables, some of which, such as an institution's financial situation, have nothing to do with a candidate's abilities. Hiring committees at other institutions are fully aware of that. So if you do not obtain tenure, you will do what many other highly competent people in that situation have done. You will obtain another position and continue with a productive career.

Meanwhile, the whole tenure process typically occurs when you are building in other areas of your life as well. You may be raising a family, buying your first house, meeting obligations to other family members, building a strong network of friendships that are deeply meaningful to you. You will not have unlimited time for these other areas of life, but don't neglect them either. Not only are they important in and of themselves, but the perspective that comes from realizing there's more to life than the next paper frequently makes the time you spend working more creative and productive.

Chapter 21
Changing Jobs

At some point you may decide or need to change jobs. There can be many reasons for changing jobs besides not being granted tenure, and each will require slightly different job-seeking strategies.

Perhaps you originally wanted to work at a different type of institution but were unable to find such a position during your original job hunt. Or, for one reason or another, you planned to stay for only a few years. Maybe you feel that the institution hasn't lived up to its original commitment to you in terms of lab space, research assistance, library funding, or something else that was negotiated during the offer. Possibly you have been approached by another institution. Possibly your partner or another family member is unhappy with the location or institution and the situation cannot be improved for him or her. If you have been conducting a long-distance marriage or relationship for several years, you may have decided that being together is more important than your job.

Be Ready for Opportunities

Continue to stay in touch with people at other institutions, even if you are very happy where you are. These contacts are a vital means of engaging in your profession. In addition, knowing faculty at other institutions gives you greater access to information about positions that may be opening up and a group of people who can comment favorably on your work.

If you got your degree from an institution that has a credentials file service, continue to build it even if you don't ever expect to move. It's a form of insurance you can draw on if you decide you must or want to change positions.

Keep your vita current. Until you are very senior you will probably continue to keep your education as the first item. However, if previously you gave a lot of detail about your graduate work, you may now begin to omit it. For at least several years after obtaining your doctorate, however, retain your dissertation topic and advisor's name. Add recent experiences and condense earlier ones. For example, if you earlier included detail about what you did as a teaching assistant, you may now merely retain the notation that you held the position. In general, it is a good idea to condense items, even if drastically, rather than to drop them altogether. Do not drop early publications and presentations.

If You Want to Make a Move

Keep in mind that academia is a small world and that if you put out feelers, chances are your department will hear about it. Mention in cover letters that you don't want your institution contacted unless you are considered a very serious contender. You will need someone to recommend you. While it is true that you can send out letters in a credentials file without the knowledge of the letters' authors, there is no guarantee that at least one of these people will not get a phone call about you. Therefore it is a better idea to speak with your recommenders, let them know what you are interested in, and ask them to keep your search confidential. Your advisor, of course, is an ideal person to play this role. It would be helpful to have a recommendation from someone in your current department. You will have to use your best judgment about the advisability of letting someone there know your plans.

If you begin interviewing extensively, it is almost inevitable that your department will learn that you are looking elsewhere. It will depend very much upon the individuals involved whether they view this as perfectly reasonable activity or a lack of commitment. In any case, it is preferable that the chair hear from you, rather than from someone else, that you are looking. You may want to defer this communication until you are almost certain that the person is about to have the information anyway. Never use the threat that you will look elsewhere as a negotiating point. If you do not find another position quickly after making such a threat, your bluff will have been called forever.

To make such a move responsibly, minimize new commitments, such as agreeing to supervise a doctoral thesis, in which your departure at year's end would seriously compromise someone else's plans.

If You Have to Move

A very common reason for changing jobs in academia is that of not getting tenure or of being very certain that it will not be awarded. Or it may be that you have accepted a short-term, nonrenewable position. In either case you will not need to keep your search quiet within the department, and you may find some very active allies there as you conduct your search.

If you felt it was likely that you would be awarded tenure and you were not, it is almost inevitable that you will feel intensely disappointed. You may also feel very angry or depressed or experience a sense of personal failure. These feelings are natural and will run their course. Try to make every effort, however, to minimize their effect on your professional behavior. If you can deal with department members and interview as if you are confident and happy about your future prospects, you will receive more positive feedback and results which, in turn, will make you genuinely feel better. Meanwhile, outside of work, take up a new activity, spend time with friends and family, seek help from a counselor, become involved in community service, or do whatever else your experience has shown you is restorative for you.

Don't lose any time in applying for jobs as soon as you find you will need to look. While you may have some impulse to avoid other department members after receiving a negative tenure decision, now is precisely the time you should be talking to them. Ask your strongest supporters if they will be willing to recommend you. Let everyone know the kinds of jobs you will be looking for, and ask people to let you know of openings they hear about. Give strongly interested and supportive people copies of your vita.

Let all your professional contacts know that you are in the market. It is most comfortable for all concerned if you take the responsibility for obtaining information. For example, rather than asking people to "keep you in mind," ask whether they can suggest whom you might call at a specific institution, what they have heard lately about a particular department, if they know someone that they might be willing to call on your behalf at an institution where you have applied, and so forth. Keep in touch about your search with those who seem enthusiastically supportive of it. If you sense that others are lukewarm, continue to keep in touch on a professional basis, but don't pursue the topic of your search with them.

When Someone Else Wants You to Move

A different kind of reason for changing jobs is that of an unsolicited advance by another institution. It's attractive to be sought out, so, if you decide to move, take your time and negotiate a good offer from the institution that is pursuing you. If you don't want to move, this is a great opportunity to give your institution a chance to keep you, through increased salary, an early, favorable tenure decision, or whatever else you might choose to negotiate for. Be aware, however, that, unless your work is truly world-class, this is an exercise you will not be able to repeat very frequently. Whenever you say, "I will take this offer unless you do X," there is a possibility that your employer will say, "We'll be sorry to lose you, but it looks as if you had best take the offer, because we certainly can't do that." As when you negotiated for your first salary, begin with open-ended questions, and don't give ultimatums unless you are willing to stand behind them.

The Graceful Exit

As soon as you have accepted an offer at another institution, let your department know. Do everything you can to tie up loose ends in terms of responsibilities to other people. If there are those in the department to whom you are genuinely grateful, be sure to express your appreciation. If you can't wait to leave every person there behind you, at a minimum, be courteous. Satisfying as you might fantasize it would be to tell everyone exactly what you think before you leave, doing so would almost certainly be something you would later regret.

After you leave, keep in touch with people with whom you have enjoyed working. The opportunity to build a rich network of contacts, to have a group of people who live all over the country, and possibly the world, whom you know you will always enjoy seeing at an annual meeting, with whom you can correspond and exchange ideas, is one of the rewards of the academic career you have chosen.

Part VI
Thinking About the
Expanded Job Market

Chapter 22
Thinking About the Expanded Job Market

Higher education is changing drastically as it becomes more market-driven. As a result, it's difficult to map out an academic career far into the future, because the rules keep changing. In almost every field in which one can obtain a Ph.D., studies show that a substantial number of people with that degree work at something other than faculty positions. Despite your best efforts, sometimes you find that events do not unfold according to plan. Perhaps your advisor is denied tenure and becomes disheartened and preoccupied halfway through your research. Perhaps you fall in love with someone rooted to a particular geographic location and you no longer are willing to move anywhere in the country. Perhaps you look at the stress your advisor is under and decide that kind of life is not for you. Perhaps the topic you were promised would be "hot" has lost its allure and you have not gotten a tenure-track job after three cycles of the job market. Whatever the specific circumstances, in many cases people who had planned to spend their careers as faculty members start to ask themselves whether that goal is attainable, or, even if it is attainable, whether it any longer seems desirable to them.

When you are considering changing fields because of limited opportunities, it becomes a very individual decision as to when you've tried "enough." In most fields there's a point of diminishing returns in the pursuit of tenure-track positions and you need to be realistic about when you've reached it. At first, the additional postdoc or short-term teaching position enhances your credentials. At some point it stops contributing anything. How long is "too long" is not the same for all fields. Find out the norm for yours so that you have some yardstick against which to measure your own perseverance. For example, many candidates in the humanities obtain a tenure-track position after a year or two of one-year appointments, but after five to ten years of one-year appointments the odds no longer favor success in finding such a job.

Even when you feel you have no options, the fact remains that people with Ph.D.s have some of the lowest unemployment rates in the country and the economy always has many places for people smart and persevering enough to earn a doctoral degree. Depending on how applied your background is, you may be able to move instantly and easily into another kind of work or it may take you a few years to make a successful transition. Everybody is marketable; the only question is how quickly so.

Learn how things work in your own field. Seeing the world in terms of tenure-track positions at four-year colleges and universities versus everything else obscures some natural connections. Some changes are more drastic than others. Nonacademic jobs are almost standard in some fields. For example, chemists frequently work in industrial research and economists frequently work at the Federal Reserve Bank. Some academics stay in academia in administrative positions. On the other hand, some people go into fields completely unpredictable from their graduate training, as when an English professor opens a restaurant or becomes a systems consultant. Some Ph.D.s consider teaching at a community college or a secondary school a career change; others don't. In some professional fields career paths may move naturally between universities and professional practice. In other fields, leaving the university is likely to be a one-way street.

Whether you are leaving the academic market because you're strongly drawn to an alternative or because you feel you have little choice, think of identifying your next career move as a major research project. Just as in your scholarly field you can't immediately write a journal article without having first framed the question and done the research, it's unlikely that you'll immediately write a successful job application without having first laid some groundwork.

Assessing Your Skills

For anyone who has spent the time required to earn a Ph.D., how much of the specialized training to use in a new career is a big decision. Some people decide they want no more to do with academic pursuits and are happy to do whatever else meets their needs, even if it has no obvious connection with their prior academic training. Others are concerned with more explicitly using their graduate education. If you find you don't want to leave your field entirely, think about what aspect of an academic career continues to appeal to you. If it's the teaching you really love, you may be inclined to look at a wider range of teaching opportunities than you had initially targeted. Or you may decide to pursue another line of work for your "main" job but continue to teach on a part-time basis. If you are most interested in research, it will depend on your field as to how many opportunities to pursue the subject are available in nonacademic settings. If you love simply being in a university, you may look at nonteaching administrative roles, such as advising, development, or administration.

If you are willing to leave the specific content of your graduate education behind you, then you can look at a wide array of options. Look back at your interests before you decided to pursue a Ph.D. Were there other interests you seriously considered which you want to investigate? While you were a graduate student or postdoc, did you develop other expertise that you found as compelling as your research? What really matters to you, and what are you really good at?

Whatever your field of study, you have much to offer that the economy rewards. What you can offer an employer includes the things you know, drawn from the content area of your field of study, specific technical and methodological skills you have mastered, more general skills, such as the ability to analyze complex data, and character traits. Content areas can be framed to meet the interests of employers. For example, research on Native American health practices could be construed as knowing something about Native Americans, about public health, or about American history. Research methods can be generalized. For example, one historian who studied the powerful individuals who governed Paris in the sixteenth century parlayed her expertise in researching individuals into a position in development research. *Outside the Ivory Tower*, by Margaret Newhouse, contains a long list of general skills which will start your thinking. Count among your assets the qualities you needed to complete your degree, such as perseverance, focus, and the ability to meet deadlines.

Identifying Alternatives and Researching Them

Many faculty members are most familiar with faculty career paths. Even if you're in a situation where you can comfortably discuss your plans with your advisor, that person may or may not be very knowledgeable about alternatives. Fortunately, there are many sources of information available.

Some books written specifically for academics who want to change careers are noted in Appendix 2. In addition, many professional associations have developed materials on their Web sites about a wide array of career alternatives. You'll find information at your campus career center and probably a good collection of links on its Web site. Your own department surely has produced some Ph.D.s who have taken nonacademic positions. Even if no formal record is kept about the whereabouts of graduates, by asking faculty and departmental administrative staff and recent graduates, you can probably identify them.

If you're fortunate, all this investigation will lead you to a clear first-choice focus for your job search in an area where you've ascertained that, with persistence, you will surely find a good job. However, it's more likely to be the case that research both uncovers interesting possibilities and, at least temporarily, further confuses you. Since you have a limited amount of time, you may need to be fairly arbitrary in deciding how you'll direct your job-search time and energy. Many people develop fairly complex decision schemes. For example, "If I can get X kind of job on the West Coast in a location my partner considers suitable for work, then I'll do that. Otherwise, if nothing comes through by February, then I'll look for Y kind of job in the Chicago area, where I'm now based."

Searching

In the academic job search you follow a fairly predictable sequence in identifying and applying for jobs. Once you think about a broader range of options, you find that there are many right ways to apply for a position, most of them highly unstructured.

Conducting academic and nonacademic job searches at the same time is difficult. Depending upon how different the nonacademic alternative is, you may need to have two sets of interview clothes and use two different vocabularies, two different sets of people to recommend you, and two different sets of job-hunting documents. Often, you will need to develop both a resume and a vita. We've included two examples of resumes, but books listed in Appendix 2 will give you more. In many cases, if you're looking for both kinds of jobs, it makes sense to concentrate on academic applications in the fall when many jobs are announced and to turn your attention to other options later in the academic year. However, if you're looking at major corporate recruiting, be aware that the corporate recruiting cycle is as early as is the academic one.

One of the best ways to job-hunt is to tell everyone what you're looking for. However, you may be in a situation in which you feel a need to keep your plans somewhat confidential. Whether you're afraid your department will be reluctant to award your degree on time if you pursue a nonacademic career or that your teaching contract won't be renewed if you're seen as lacking commitment, there are some real, in addition to imagined, risks to announcing plans that are different from those that key people expect you to have. How you resolve this dilemma is a judgment call; however, it will definitely take you longer to make a career change if you can't discuss your plans and immediate goals with someone.

There are several potential sources of good career consultation, although you may need to try more than one until you find a source that seems credible. If you're finishing a degree, a good place to start is with your campus career center. However, it may or may not be very familiar with the situations of doctoral students. Since many career centers provide alumni services, your undergraduate institution is another option, as is the career center at an institution where you may be teaching. Career centers which don't provide service to doctoral candidates can sometimes provide referrals to private counselors who have worked with Ph.D.s.

Also check with your scholarly or professional association. Nearly all associations provide at least some career services for their members. While it's the exception rather than the rule, some have staff members who can advise members on applying their skills in new fields. Others have provided Web sites with an interactive mentor feature.

You may consider working with career counselors and career counseling services operating on a for-profit basis. A new related service being widely offered is professional coaching. The quality of such services varies wildly. Avoid those who charge a large up-front fee and look for those who have had experience working not just with career changers in general, but with academics in particular.

While there are several steps you must take to make a successful career transition, they aren't necessarily sequential. You may find, for example, that you originally identify a career goal which proves impossible to achieve. Then you may need to return to your self-assessment and research. Or you may have an interview for a job for which you are turned down, but where the interviewer suggests that you interview the next day for something related. In that case, you may need to jump ahead to the application and catch up on research later. It's important both to develop goals and to remain flexible as you pursue them. Even though you end up doing something you never imagined when you began your doctoral study, it's likely that the result of your nontraditional search will be work that is rewarding and that uses the skills you've developed over the years you pursued an academic career.

Appendices

Appendix 1: National Job Listing Sources and Scholarly and Professional Associations

Periodicals That Include Job Listings of Interest to Scholars in All Fields

Black Issues in Higher Education
published every two weeks (26 issues per year)

Cox Matthews & Associates, Inc.
10520 Warwick Ave., Suite B-8
Fairfax, VA 22030
800–783–3199, 703–385–2981; 703–385–1839 (fax);

This magazine covers a wide range of issues in higher education and how they affect African Americans and minorities. An annual special report covers careers in higher education, including salaries. Many pages of each issue are devoted to faculty and administration position announcements from institutions across the United States and abroad.

The Chronicle of Higher Education/Career Network
published weekly (49 issues per year)

1255 23rd St., N.W.
Washington, DC 20037
202–466–1000; 202–296–2691 (fax); <www.chronicle.com>

This is the newspaper of higher education. Articles cover all aspects of teaching, research, administration, and student life. The focus is on American higher education with additional coverage on the rest of the world. Grant deadlines, faculty promotions, and book reviews are included.

The "Career Network," the *Chronicle's* recruitment service, has extensive listings for faculty and administrative position announcements from institutions worldwide, although primarily from those in the United States. Announcements are listed in two ways: an alphabetical listing by subject and display ads with an accompanying index. The *Chronicle* is also available on-line at <www.chronicle.com>. The free on-line Career Network site also features a wide array of editorial content relating to the academic market and job searches. See "Career Talk" for a monthly column by Mary Morris Heiberger and Julia Miller Vick.

Selected Scholarly and Professional Associations

Many associations include job listings in the association newsletter, which can also include grant deadlines, information on conferences, news of members, and short news articles. Some associations have a separate job listing available to members and nonmembers for an additional charge. Some associations produce both kinds of publications. It is often possible to have job listings sent first class for an additional fee. Increasingly, associations also post funding and job announcements on a Web site as well. Sometimes announcements are password-secured for association members.

For each association listed here you will find the association name, address, phone number, fax number, electronic addresses when available, discipline(s) it serves, title and frequency of job listing publications, time of the annual convention, description of convention placement services, and title of its discipline-specific handout on job hunting if there is one. If the organizations relevant to your discipline are not listed here, consult *National Trade and Professional Associations of the United States 2000*, ed. Buck Downs; *The Scholarly Societies Project* at <www.scholarly-societies.org>, and your advisor.

Academy of Management
P.O. Box 3020
Briarcliff Manor, NY 10510–3020
914–923–2607; 914–923–2615 (fax); academy@pace.edu;

Management

Placement services are available on the Web. If you do not have a membership, enter as a guest. With membership, you can post your resume and teaching preferences.

Convention is held in August. In order to attend, membership is required. Placement services (interviewing space) are made available during the convention.

African Studies Association
Rutgers, The State University of New Jersey
Douglass Campus, 132 George Street
New Brunswick, NJ 08901–1400
732–932–8173; 732–932–3394 (fax); callASA@rci.rutgers.edu;
<www.africanstudies.org>

African Studies

ASA News is issued quarterly.

Annual conference is held in November.

American Academy of Religion
825 Houston Mill Rd., NE
Atlanta, GA 30329–4246
404–727–3049; 404–727–7959 (fax); aar@aarweb.org; <www.aarweb.org>

Religious Studies, Theology, Ministry

Openings: Job Opportunities for Scholars of Religion is issued 12 times a year to members of the American Academy of Religion and the Society of Biblical Literature and made available online.

Annual meeting is held in November (weekend before Thanksgiving). Employment Information Services center provides interview space. Interviews set up by employers and candidates.

American Anthropological Association
4350 North Fairfax Drive, Suite 640
Arlington, VA 22203
703–528–1902; 703–528–3546 (fax); placement@aaanet.org;
<www./aaanet.org/>

Anthropology

Anthropology News is issued 9 times a year to members. *Placement Service Notes,* 10 issues per year, includes job listings. Jobs are also listed online.

Convention is usually held in November. Job listings (free for members) are posted and persons can apply at the convention. Space is provided for convention interviewing.

American Astronomical Society
2000 Florida Ave., N.W., Suite 400
Washington, DC 20009
202–328–2010; 202–234–2560 (fax); aas@aas.org;

Astronomy, Astrophysics

Jobs are listed in the *American Astronomical Society Job Register* (either electronically or in hard copy), issued monthly to members and also posted on the association's Web site.

Meetings are usually held in winter and summer. A Job Center, set up to get applicants and employers together, is available for members and nonmembers.

American Chemical Society
1155 16th St., N.W.
Washington, DC 20036
202–872–4600; 202–872–4615 (fax); career@acs.org; <www.acs.org>

Chemistry, Chemical Engineering

ChemJobs, an online database of job listings, is free to members, with no access to nonmembers. The weekly *Chemical & Engineering News* (*C&EN*) carries the same ads.

National meetings are held twice a year, usually around March/August, and include the Career Resource Center.

American Economic Association
2014 Broadway, Suite 305
Nashville, TN 37203
615–22–2595; 615–43–7590 (fax); <www.vanderbilt.edu/AEA/index.htm>

Economics

Job Openings for Economists, published 10 times a year, is available to members and nonmembers by subscription.

Convention is held in January each year. A placement service can be contacted at 312–793–4904.

American Educational Research Association
1230 17th St., N.W.
Washington, DC 20036–3078
202–223–9485; 202–775–1824 (fax); <www.aera.net>

Education

Educational Researcher is published 9 times a year for members and accessible online, at AERA's Web site. Job openings are listed in its classified section.

Convention is held in the spring. Interview facilities are made available.

American Folklore Society
c/o American Anthropological Association
4350 North Fairfax Drive, Suite 640
Arlington, VA 22203
703–528–1902; 703–528–3546 (fax);

Folklore and Folklife

AFSNews is issued bimonthly to members.

Annual convention is held in October.

American Historical Association
400 A St., S.E.
Washington, DC 20003
202–544–2422; 202–544–8307 (fax);

History, Ancient History, American Studies, and other area studies, and history professionals such as archivists and librarians.

Perspectives is issued monthly during the academic year to members.

Convention is held in January. Job Register enables departments to register for interviewing space at the annual meeting.

Publishes *Careers for Students in History*.

American Institute of Biological Sciences
1444 Eye St., N.W., Suite 200
Washington, DC 20005
202–628–1500; 202–628–1509 (fax); Washington@AIBS.org; <www.aibs.org>

Biology (does not include Medical Biology or Biotechnology)

BioScience, a monthly publication, includes job listings. Jobs are also posted to the association's Web site.

Annual meeting is held in March.

Publishes *Careers in Biology*.

American Institute of Chemical Engineers
3 Park Ave.
New York, NY 10016–5991
800-AIChemE; 212–591–8100; 212–591–8888 (fax); express@aiche.org;
<www.aiche.org>

Chemical Engineering

The Institute offers an electronic job-posting service;
also a toll-free number, 800–803–3446 for career/employment services.

Convention is held twice a year.

American Institute of Physics
One Physics Ellipse
College Park, MD 20740
301–209–3190; 301–209–0841 (fax); aipinfo@aip.org; <www.aip.org>

Physics

Job Opportunities, an online searchable jobs database, lists hundreds of job openings each month. Job openings are updated daily.

Employment centers are offered at AIP at member and affiliated society meetings. AIP also manages employment for the American Physical Society.

American Mathematical Society
Box 6248
Providence, RI 02940
800–321–4AMS; 401–455–4000; 401–331–3842 (fax); ams@ams.org;
<www.ams.org>

Mathematics

Notices of the American Mathematical Society is issued monthly to all members. *Employment Information in the Mathematical Sciences* is issued 7 times a year, extra charge for members and nonmembers. Ads can be browsed for free on Web site.

Convention is held in January. Employment Register organizes formal interviewing.

Publishes *The Academic Job Search in Mathematics.*

American Musicological Society
201 S. 34th St.
Philadelphia, PA 19104–6313
215–898–8698; 888–611–4AMS; 215–573–3673(fax);
ams@sas.upenn.edu;

Music

Newsletter *AMS News* is given as part of membership.

Convention is held in October or November.

American Philological Association
291 Logan Hall
University of Pennsylvania
249 S. 36th Street
Philadelphia, PA 19104–6304
215–898–4975; 215–573–7874 (fax); apaclassics@sas.upenn.edu;
<www.apaclassics.org>

Classical Studies, Greek and Latin Languages, Classical Archaeology, Ancient History, Linguistics

Positions for Classicists and Archaeologists, is provided monthly and online.

Convention is usually held in early January. Interviews are scheduled by the association.

Publishes *Careers for Classicists.*

American Philosophical Association
University of Delaware
31 Amstel Avenue
Newark, DE 19716
302–831–1112; 302–831–8690 (fax); apaOnline@udel.edu; <www.udel.edu/apa>

Philosophy

Jobs for Philosophers is provided 4 times a year to members only.

Three conventions a year are held: Eastern Division in December (largest), Pacific Division in March, Central Division in May. A placement service is held at each one, through a mailbox system. Candidates leave vitas along with interview requests. Institutions respond to them, usually for an interview during the convention.

American Planning Association
1776 Massachusetts Ave., N.W.
Suite 400
Washington, DC 20036
202–872–0611; 202–872–0643 (fax); CareerInfo@planning.org;

City and Regional Planning

JobMart is published 22 times a year. *JobsOnline* is also available.

Annual convention is held in March or April.

American Political Science Association
1527 New Hampshire Ave., N.W.
Washington, DC 20036
202–483–2512; 202–483–2657 (fax); apsa@apsanet.org; <www.apsanet.org>

Political Science, International Relations, Government, Public Administration, Public Policy

APSA Personnel Service Newsletter, monthly and online, is open only to members by subscription.

Convention is held the Thursday before Labor Day. Interviewing space is available.

American Psychological Association
750 First St., N.E.
Washington, DC 20002–4242
800–374–2721; 202–336–5500; 202–336–6069 (fax); convention@apa.org;

Psychology

APA Monitor on Psychology is sent monthly to members and ads are online.

Convention is held in August and includes interviewing opportunities.

American Society for Microbiology
1752 N Street, N.W.
Washington, DC 20036
202–737–3600; 202–942–9367 (fax); subscriptions@asmusa.org;

ASM News employment classified ads for members only, are updated monthly.

ASM's annual general meetings are held in the late spring. ASM Job Match is for members only.

American Society for Public Administration
1120 G Street, N.W., Suite 700
Washington, DC 20005
(202) 393–7878; (202) 638–4952 (fax); info@aspanet.org; <www.aspanet.org>

Public Administration

The Recruiter Online is available on the association's Web site.

Conference is held in March and includes a job fair.

American Society of Civil Engineers
World Headquarters
1801 Alexander Bell Drive
Reston, VA 20191–4400
703–295–6000; 703–295–6333 (fax); <www.asce.org>

Civil Engineering

ASCE News, monthly newspaper, lists positions available and is also online.

Convention is held in October.

American Sociological Association
1307 New York Avenue, N.W., Suite 700
Washington, DC 20005
202–383–9005; 202–638–0882 (fax); executive.office@asanet.org;
<www.asanet.org>

Sociology

Employment Bulletin, monthly, is available online at no charge, print edition for additional charge.

Convention is held in August. Employers submit job descriptions and set up interviews.

American Statistical Association
1429 Duke St.
Alexandria, VA 22314–3402
703–684–1221; 703–584–2037 (fax); asainfo@asa.mhs.compuserv.com;
<www.amstat.org>

Statistics

AMSTAT News is available monthly to members and available to nonmembers for an additional charge.

Convention is held in August. Employers and applicants preregister for placement service.

American Studies Association
1120 19th St., N.W., Suite 301
Washington, DC 20036
202–467–4783; 202–467–4786 (fax); asastaff@erols.com;
<www.georgetown.edu/crossroads/asainfo.html>

American Studies, English, History

ASA Newsletter is sent quarterly to members.

Convention is held in the fall and serves as a job clearinghouse; job listings are also online.

Archaeological Institute of America
Boston University
656 Beacon St.
Boston, MA 02215–2006
617–353–9361; 617–353–6550 (fax); aia@bu.edu; <www.archaeological.org>

Archaeology, Classical Studies

American Journal of Archaeology is published quarterly in print and electronic formats for members and by subscription.

The convention is held in January and includes a placement service.

Associated Writing Programs
Tallwood House, Mail Stop 1E3
George Mason University
Fairfax, VA 22030
703–993–4301; 703–993–4302 (fax); awp@gmu.edu;

English, Writing

AWP Job List is issued 7 times a year to members. Job listings are also posted on a password-protected Web site for members. Career Placement Service (a dossier-mailing service) is also available to members only.

Association for Asian Studies
1021 East Huron Street
Ann Arbor, MI 48104
734–665–2490; 734–665–3801 (fax); postmaster@aasianst.org;

China and Inner Asia Studies, Northeast Asia Studies, South Asia Studies, and Southeast Asia Studies

"Personnel Registry" provided in *Asian Studies Newsletter*, is issued 4 times a year to members. Job listings are also posted (and updated more often) on the Web site.

Convention is held in the spring; candidates and employers can register and set up interviews.

Association for Theatre in Higher Education
P.O. Box 4537
Boulder, CO 80306–4537
888–284–3737; 303–440–0851; 303–440–0852 (fax);
Nericksn@aol.com; <www.hawaii.edu/athe>

Theatre

ATHENEWS, the association's newsletter, is printed three times a year, for members. It is also available online.

The convention is held in July or August.

Association of Collegiate Schools of Architecture
1735 New York Ave., N.W., 3rd Floor
Washington, DC 20006
202–785–2324; 202–628–0448 (fax);

Architecture

ACSA News is issued monthly during the academic year.

The annual meeting is usually held in March.

The Association for Education in Journalism and Mass Communication
234 Outlet Pointe Blvd., Suite A
Columbia, SC 29210–5667
803–798–0271; 803–772–3509 (fax); aejmc@aejmc.org; <www.aejmc.org>

Journalism, Communications, Public Relations, Advertising

AEJMC News is issued 6 times a year to members. Jobs are also posted on the AEJMC Web site.

The convention is held in August; job listings, resume books, and interviewing are available.

College Art Association
275 Seventh Ave.
New York, NY 10001
212–691–1051; 212–627–2381 (fax); nyoffice@collegeart.org;
<www.collegeart.org>

Fine Arts (Studio), Art History

Job listings, *CAA Careers*, is issued 6 times a year to individual institutional members. Some job listings are on the Web site.

The convention is normally held in late February. Interviewing space is made available for members.

Council on Social Work Education
1725 Duke St., Suite 500
Alexandria, VA 22314
703–683–8080; 703–683–8099 (fax); info@cswe.org; <www.cswe.org>

Social Work

Teachers Registry and Information Service, is provided 3 times a year to those who sign up for the service.

The convention is held in March. Job listings and vitas are made available.

Federation of American Societies for Experimental Biology
9650 Rockville Pike
Bethesda, MD 20814–3998
301–530–7020; 301–571–0699 (fax); career@faseb.org;
<https://ns2.faseb.org/careerweb>

Biomedical, Behavioral, and Pharmaceutical Sciences

CAREERS OnLine CLASSIFIED, a weekly Internet-accessible listing of employment opportunities and positions wanted within the biomedical, behavioral, and pharmaceutical professions, is updated weekly. *CAREERS OnLine DataNet*, an Internet-accessible database of employment opportunities and applicant profile data, lets applicants list profile data at no cost.

FASEB Placement Service provides employers the opportunity to meet and interview qualified applicants for available employment opportunities. FASEB manages approximately 12 meetings and 24 conferences annually.

Federation member and associate member societies include:

American Association of Anatomists, 301–530–8314
American Association of Immunologists, 301–530–7178
American Physiological Society, 301–530–7118
American Peptide Society
American Society for Biochemistry and Molecular Biology, 301–530–7145
American Society for Bone and Mineral Research, 202–367–1161
American Society for Cell Biology, 301–347–9300
American Society for Clinical Investigation, 856–608–1105
American Society of Human Genetics, 301–571–1825
American Society for Investigative Pathology, 301–530–7130
American Society for Nutritional Sciences, 301–530–7050
American Society for Pharmacology and Experimental Therapeutics,
    301–530–7060
Association of Biomolecular Resource Facilities, 505–983–8102
Biophysical Society, 301–530–7114
Endocrine Society, 301–941–0200
Protein Society, 301–571–0662
Radiation Research Society, 630–571–2881
Society for Developmental Biology, 301–571–0647
Society for Gynecologic Investigation, 202–863–2544
Society for the Study of Reproduction, 608–256–2777
Teratology Society, 703–438–3104

Geological Society of America
Box 9140
Boulder, CO 80301–9140
303–447–2020, 800–472–1988; 303–447–1133 (fax); <www.geosociety.org>

Geology

GSA Today is issued monthly to members. Job listings are also available on the Web site.

Convention is normally held in the fall. Vitas can be input into a computer database. Space for interviewing is provided.

Gerontological Society of America
1030 15th Street, N.W., Suite 250
Washington, DC 20005–4006
202–842–1275; 202–842–1150 (fax); geron@geron.org;

Social Gerontology, Sociology

Gerontology News, monthly to members, is available to nonmembers for a charge. Jobs are also listed online.

Convention is held in November. Free job and resume postings are available on site. Individuals make their own arrangements for interviews.

History of Science Society
University of Washington
Box 351330
Seattle, WA 98195–1330
206–43–9366; 206–85–9544 (fax); hssexec@u.washington.edu;
<http://depts.washington.edu/hssexec/>

History and Sociology of Science and Medicine

Newsletter is issued quarterly to membership. Employment opportunity listings are on its Web site.

Convention is held in the fall, usually early November. Interviewing space is made available.

Institute of Electrical and Electronics Engineers, Inc. (IEEE)
445 Hoes Lane
P.O. Box 1331
Piscataway, NJ 08855–1331
732–981–0060; 732–981–9667 (fax); <www.ieee.org>
Electrical/Electronics Engineering

Job search service is available for free on IEEE Web site.

The IEEE hosts more than 300 conferences and meetings each year.

International Communication Association
8140 Burnet Road, P.O. Box 9589
Austin, TX 78766
512–454–8299; 512–451–6270 (fax); icahdq@uts.cc.utexas.edu;
<www.icahdq.org>

Communication

ICA Newsletter is issued bimonthly to members. Classified ads are available on the ICA Web site.

The convention is held in late spring to midsummer.

Latin American Studies Association
946 William Pitt Union
University of Pittsburgh
Pittsburgh, PA 15260
412–648–7929; 412–624–7145; lasa+@pitt.edu;
<http://lasa.international.pitt.edu>

Latin American Studies

LASA Forum is issued quarterly and includes employment opportunities. Employment opportunities are also posted to the association's Web site.

Linguistic Society of America
1325 18th St., N.W., Suite 211
Washington, DC 20036–6501
202–835–1714; 202–835–1717 (fax); lsa@lsadc.org;

Linguistics

"Job Opportunities" is part of the *LSA Bulletin,* issued a minimum of 4 times a year to members.

Convention is held in January. Announcements and vitas are collected and space is made available for interviewing.

Materials Research Society
506 Keystone Drive
Warrendale, PA 15086–7573
724–779–3003; 724–779–8313 (fax); info@mrs.org; <www.mrs.org>

Materials Science

MRS Bulletin is issued monthly to members and is available on the Web site.

Two conventions are held: West Coast in spring, East Coast in fall. Members' benefits include career services such as the Job Placement Center at MRS meetings.

Modern Language Association of America
26 Broadway, 3rd Floor
New York, NY 10004–1789
646–576–5000; 646–458–0300 (fax); info@mla.org; <www.mla.org>

English, Comparative Literature, Modern Languages and Literatures

Job Information List, is issued 4 times a year for a separate charge, and on the MLA Web site. Graduate students and faculty in member departments of the Association of Departments of English and Association of Departments of Foreign Languages have free access to the online *JIL* through the ADE <www.ade.org> and ADFL <www.adfl.org> Web sites.

Convention is held in December and interviews can be scheduled.

National League for Nursing
61 Broadway, #33rd Floor
New York, NY 10006
212–363–5555 or 800–669–1656; 212–812–0393 (fax);
inform@nln.org;

Nursing

Nursing and Health Care Perspective is issued 6 times a year. Classified ads are also on the NLN Web site, available to nonmembers for a separate charge.

Annual Education Summit is usually held in September or early October, and exhibitors and representatives from nursing professions come and talk with students.

National Women's Studies Association
University of Maryland
7100 Baltimore Blvd., Suite 500
College Park, MD 20740
301-403-0525; 301-403-4137 (fax): nwsa@umail.umd.edu; <www.nwsa.org>

Women's Studies

JOBS in Women's Studies is available on the Web site.

Annual conference is held in June. A Job Fair area is available for posting information about jobs as well as for interviewing.

Population Association of America
8630 Fenton Street, Suite 722
Silver Spring, MD 20910–3812
301–565–6710; 301–565–7850 (fax); info@popassoc.org;

Demography

Members receive *Demography*, the association's quarterly journal. Job announcements are available for free on its Web site. *PAA Affairs*, a newsletter issued quarterly to members, is available by subscription to nonmembers.

Convention is held in the spring, includes Employment Exchange.

Regional Science Association International
University of Illinois
Bevier Hall, Room 83
905 S. Goodwin Ave.
Urbana, IL 61801–3682
217–333–8904; 217–333–3065 (fax); rsai@uiuc.edu; <http://rsai.geography.ohio-state.edu/rsai>

Regional Science

RSAI News, the association's newsletter, is issued 3 times a year to members. Job announcements are available on the association's Web site.

Society for Industrial and Applied Mathematics
3600 University City Science Center
Philadelphia, PA 19104–2688
215–382–9800; 215–386–7999 (fax); service@siam.org; <www.siam.org>

Mathematics

SIAM News is published 10 times per year; nonmembers may subscribe. Additional opportunities are posted only to the Web.

Annual conference is held in July.

Discipline Index to Major Scholarly Associations

Scholarly associations exist for other disciplines not listed here and disciplines listed here may additionally be served by associations not listed above.

American Studies: American Historical Association, American Studies Association

Ancient History: American Historical Association, American Philological Association

Anthropology: American Anthropological Association

Archaeology: Archaeological Institute of America

Architecture: Association of Collegiate Schools of Architecture

Area Studies: African Studies Association, American Historical Association, Association for Asian Studies, Latin American Studies Association

Art History: College Art Association of America

Astronomy: American Astronomical Society

Astrophysics: American Astronomical Society

Biology: American Institute of Biological Sciences

Chemistry: American Chemical Society

City Planning: American Planning Association

Classical Archaeology: Archaeological Institute of America

Classical Languages: American Philological Association

Communications: Association for Education in Journalism and Mass Communication, International Communication Association

Comparative Literature: Modern Language Association of America

Demography: Population Association of America

Economics: American Economic Association

Education: American Educational Research Association

Engineering: American Chemical Society, American Physical Society, Institute of Electrical and Electronics Engineers, American Society of Civil Engineers, American Institute of Chemical Engineers, Materials Research Society

English: American Studies Association, Associated Writing Programs, Modern Language Association of America

Fine Arts: College Art Association of America

Folklore and Folklife: American Folklore Society

Geology: Geological Society of America

Gerontology: Gerontological Society of America

Government: American Political Science Association

Greek: American Philological Association

History: American Historical Association, American Studies Association

History of Science: History of Science Society

International Relations: American Political Science Association

Journalism: Association of Schools of Journalism and Mass Communication

Languages/Literature, Modern: Modern Language Association of America

Latin: American Philological Association

Linguistics: American Philological Association, Linguistics Society of America, Modern Language Association of America

Management: Academy of Management

Materials Science: Materials Research Society

Mathematics: American Mathematical Society, Society for Industrial and Applied Mathematics

Music: American Musicological Society

Nursing: National League for Nursing

Philosophy: American Philosophical Association

Physics: American Institute of Physics, American Physical Society (See entry for AIP.)

Political Science: American Political Science Association

Public Affairs: American Society for Public Administration

Psychology: American Psychological Association

Regional Planning: American Planning Association

Regional Science: Regional Science Association International

Religious Studies: American Academy of Religion

Social Work: Council on Social Work Education

Sociology: American Sociological Association

Statistics: American Statistical Association

Theatre: Association for Theatre in Higher Education

Theology: American Academy of Religion

Women's Studies: National Women's Studies Association

Appendix 2: Additional Reading

This selective listing is provided to give you ideas about the type of additional reading that may help you in your job search. It is not intended to be a comprehensive bibliography. For current articles on topics such as the job market in your field, trends in higher education, and academic life, consult your professional association and library and on-line indices to publications.

General

Boufis, Christina and Victoria C. Olsen, eds. *On the Market: Surviving the Academic Job Search.* New York: Riverhead Books, 1997.
    This collection of first-person accounts gives a realistic perspective on what to expect in an academic job search.

Caplan, Paula J. *Lifting a Ton of Feathers: A Woman's Guide to Surviving in the Academic World.* Toronto: University of Toronto Press, 1994.
    After outlining myths and catch-22s, the author discusses general and specific suggestions for women from the time they enter graduate school through retirement from academia.

DeNeef, A. Leigh and Craufurd D. Goodwin, eds. *The Academic's Handbook.* 2nd ed. Durham, N.C.: Duke University Press, 1995.
    Chapters written by several professors describe the structure of the academic career and the life of an academic. Sections cover academic employment, teaching, getting funding, and publishing.

Dews, C. L. Barney and Carolyn Leste Law, eds. *This Fine Place So Far from Home: Voices of Academics from the Working Class.* Philadelphia: Temple University Press, 1995.
    This collection of first-person essays by successful academics for whom entering the professoriate meant moving between social classes includes many essays by scholars from minority groups which are underrepresented in higher education.

Ferber, Marianne A. and Jane W. Loeb, eds. *Academic Couples: Problems and Promises.* Champaign-Urbana: University of Illinois Press, 1997.

Sixteen experts examine the special challenges faced and presented by academic couples, both from the perspective of the individuals involved and from that of educational institutions.

Jones, Lee, ed., foreword by Na'im Akbar. *Brothers of the Academy: Up and Coming Black Scholars Earning Our Way in Higher Education.* Sterling, Va.: Stylus, 2000.
   Twenty-seven essays by black male scholars present first-person and historical and sociological perspectives.

McNaron, Toni A. H. *Poisoned Ivy: Lesbian and Gay Academics Confronting Homophobia.* Philadelphia: Temple University Press, 1997.
   This volume is based on both the author's first-hand experience and on a survey of 300 lesbian and gay academics with at least 15 years in their profession.

Phillips, Gerald M. and Dennis S. Gouran, Scott A. Kuehn, and Julia T. Wood. *Survival in the Academy: A Guide for Beginning Academics.* Cresskill, N.J.: Hampton, 1994.
   Written by four professors for the Speech Communication Association, this book is on life as an academic, including teaching, research, and criticism. Of special interest to job seekers are chapters on securing a position, starting out, and professionalism.

Toth, Emily. *Ms. Mentor's Impeccable Advice for Women in Academia.* Philadelphia: University of Pennsylvania Press, 1997.
   The author offers witty and on-target practical advice about resolving a variety of dilemmas. A great deal of the commonsense information is actually quite relevant to men, as well as to women.

Humanities/Arts

Gustafson, Melanie S., ed. *Becoming a Historian: A Survival Manual for Women and Men.* Washington, D.C.: American Historical Association, 2001.
   This guide focuses on the job search. It has an interesting chapter on "The Professional Couple" and an extensive discussion on "Getting Published."

Showalter, English, Howard Figler, Lori G. Kletzer, Jack H. Schuster, and Seth R. Katz. *The MLA Guide to the Job Search: A Handbook for Departments and Ph.D.s and Ph.D. Candidates in English and Foreign Languages.* New York: Modern Language Association, 1996.
   This is a comprehensive guide for language and literature Ph.D.s. The chapter on "The Academic Job Search" is extensive. One section addresses experienced candidates. The *Guide* also includes chapters on community and junior colleges and advice to departments.

For a useful Web site, see the *Humanities at Work: The Doctorate Beyond the Academy* <www.woodrow.org/phd>. The site contains links also useful to social scientists.

Science/Engineering

Feibelman, Peter J. *A Ph.D. Is Not Enough: A Guide to Survival in Science.* Reading, Mass.: Addison-Wesley, 1993.
   The author suggests science survival skills useful from the beginning of graduate school on through one's career. Chapter 5 covers academic and industrial career choices and chapter 6 deals with job interviews, including responding to offers.

Fiske, Peter S. and Aaron Louis (illustrator). *Put Your Science to Work: The Take-Charge Career Guide for Scientists.* Washington, D.C.: American Geophysical Union, 2000.
   This book is a complete revision of Fiske's earlier work *To Boldly Go: A Practical Career Guide for Scientists.* It includes practical advice for finding traditional jobs in science as well as other options. In providing sample resumes and cover letters and stories of scientists who have moved into a variety of careers it informs the reader of many career possibilities.

Reis, Richard M. *Tomorrow's Professor: Preparing for Academic Careers in Science and Engineering.* New York: IEEE Press, 1997.
   This volume includes both general strategies and individual vignettes and stories.

Rosen, Stephen and Celia Paul. *Career Renewal: Tools for Scientists and Technical Professionals.* San Diego, Calif.: Academic Press, 1997.
   Useful to anyone seeking to change career direction, the book includes both success stories and do-it-yourself exercises.

Social Sciences

Boice, Robert. *Advice for New Faculty Members: Nihil Nimus.* Needham Heights, Mass.: Allyn and Bacon, 2000.
   This book includes suggestions, not only on getting started in teaching, but also about establishing the writing schedule and human relationships which will increase the chances of achieving tenure.

Diamond, Robert M. *Preparing for Promotion and Tenure Review: A Faculty Guide.* Bolton: Anker Publishing Co., 1995.
   This volume is on the American Sociological Association's publication list.

Frost, Peter J. and M. Susan Taylor, eds. *Rhythms of Academic Life: Personal Accounts of Careers in Academia.* Thousand Oaks, Calif.: Sage Publications, 1996.
   A large compendium of essays by scholars, the book examines both traditional and non-traditional career paths and the role and future of business schools in higher education.

Menges, Robert J. *Faculty in New Jobs: A Guide to Settling In, Becoming Established, and Building Institutional Support.* San Francisco: Jossey-Bass Higher and Adult Education Series, 1999.

This collection of essays by a variety of scholars draws on a study conducted by the National Center on Postsecondary Teaching, Learning, and Assessment.

Rheingold, Harriet L. *The Psychologist's Guide to an Academic Career.* Washington, D.C.: American Psychological Association, 1994.
This very comprehensive guide offers advice about graduate study, the job search, and getting established in and developing an academic career. Much of the advice is relevant to scholars in related disciplines.

The Expanded Market

Debelius, Maggie and Susan Elizabeth Basalla. *So What Are You Going to Do With That? A Guide for M.A.'s and Ph.D.'s Seeking Careers Outside the Academy.* New York: Farrar Straus & Giroux, 2001.
This volume is aimed at the graduate student who is questioning whether to finish the graduate program and seek an academic career. People who have left the academy for a variety of options are profiled. Also included are self-assessment tools, interviewing tips, and suggestions for repackaging one's academic experience.

Kreeger, Karen Young. *Guide to Nontraditional Careers in Science.* Philadelphia: Taylor & Francis, 1999.
This very comprehensive guide both describes a variety of career options for scientists and provides detailed resource information for learning more about them.

Newhouse, Margaret. *Outside the Ivory Tower: A Guide for Academics Considering Alternative Careers.* Cambridge, Mass.: Office of Career Services, Harvard University, 1993.
This book suggests how Ph.D.s may assess their skills and explore the wide variety of nonacademic careers. Two particularly useful features are a lengthy list of skills graduate students may have developed and a chart relating them to career fields.

Robbins-Roth, Cynthia, ed. *Alternative Careers in Science: Leaving the Ivory Tower.* San Diego, Calif.: Academic Press, 1998.
A series of first-person accounts profiles a variety of alternatives for Ph.D. scientists.

Sindermann, Carl J. and Thomas K. Sawyer. *The Scientist as Consultant: Building New Career Opportunities.* New York: Plenum Press, 1999.
For scientists at all career levels, this book describes the many issues to be attended to by a scientist who hopes to establish an independent consulting practice.

Also noteworthy is *Science's Next Wave,* <www.nextwave.org> an online journal published by the American Association for the Advancement of Science. Its growing archival collection includes materials on both traditional and nontraditional careers for scientists.

Index